# ST SERAPHIM OF SAROV

# St Seraphim of Sarov

Valentine Zander

Translated by

Sister Gabriel Anne S.S.C

Introduction by

Father Boris Bobrinskoy

Library of Congress Cataloging-in-Publication Data

Zander, Valentine.
    St Seraphim of Sarov
    German translation has title: Seraphim von Sarow.
    Biblography: p.
    1.    Serafim, Saint, 1759-1833. I. Title
BX597.S37Z33    1975    281.9'092'4    [B]    75-42136
ISBN 0-913836-28-1

# St Seraphim of Sarov

Originally published in German under the title:
*Seraphim von Sarow.*

© 1975 by Valentine Zander

English Translation © 1975 by
The Society for Promoting Christian Knowledge

This edition produced by permission.

St Vladimir's Seminary Press
575 Scarsdale Road
Crestwood, New York 10707
www.svspress.com    800-204-2665

ISBN 978-0-913836-28-6

PRINTED IN THE UNITED STATES OF AMERICA

# Contents

## Contents

# Introduction

BY FATHER BORIS BOBRINSKOY

To reveal Staretz Seraphim, or rather to make him come alive alongside the pages of this book, is the whole aim of Valentine Zander's work. It is concerned not so much with a new study of Orthodox holiness nor with St Seraphim's teaching on the Holy Spirit—there is no lack of such writings among our contemporary literature—as to fill a need, to present to western readers an authentic biography of St Seraphim in which the author's own personality effaces itself as much as possible in order to let the Staretz himself speak and live before our eyes.

Many have felt the crying need for such a biography, because it is very important to see St Seraphim in the situations and time in which he was set, and not to disembody him in a timeless existence; though this may be at the risk of astonishing and even scandalizing the 'modern' reader: it may seem all wrong to him to see the supernatural and miraculous come bursting in and overwhelming ordinary life.

One of the most striking characteristics of Staretz Seraphim is surely that intimacy with the Mother of God which is discernible throughout his life. This intimacy seems remarkable to me even within the history of Orthodox holiness. St Seraphim is a singular example both of predilection on Mary's part and of veneration on his, of instructions given both to him and to his community, of that constant, tangible intimacy which sometimes manifests itself in the smallest details of his spiritual warfare, in his period of *startchestvo* (direction) or in his administration of the convent of 'orphans' of Diveyevo which was specially protected by Mary. This is not the place to relate the details of those interventions of the Mother of God in Seraphim's life; they are faithfully delineated in Valentine Zander's work. St Seraphim's Marial piety represents to a high degree the traditional sense of a shared experience in a fervent people's everyday life, that is, the presence and motherly intercession of the Most Pure Virgin.

The content of the Staretz' spiritual message consists precisely in reminding a post-Christian world filled with its own sufficiency that the mystery of the Church is a mystery of continuity and true communication between, on the one hand, the life of God and of his saints and, on the other, our daily experience of prayer and sanctification.

It is at this level of experience and spiritual vision that we are to consider the essential message of St Seraphim's life, the mystery of the Holy Spirit. When we invoke the Mother of the Saviour· and all those who, following after her, have become living temples of the Spirit we attain to the real work, the personal coming of the Spirit who, in contrast to the Son, does not communicate his hypostasis (Person) to the Church but who hides himself, identifies himself as it were, with human persons in whom he appropriates the deifying energies of the Trinity. She who was the chosen dwelling-place of the Holy Spirit at the time of the incarnation of her Son participates with her motherly intercession in our own growing into the Holy Spirit and our divine filiation. Therefore it is at this same level and in a profoundly reciprocal causality that we are to place St Seraphim's familiarity with the Mother of God, his charismatic illumination, and his own teaching about the Holy Spirit.

In all periods of his history man has been sensitive to the Spirit's breath; through an intuitive, inward sense he recognizes those who are the bearers and the chosen of the Spirit. Perhaps our generation is particularly marked, in all Christian confessions, by a profound seeking, a rediscovery, a return to awareness of the Holy Spirit.

So St Seraphim's illumination and his spiritual message have come at their proper time. He is a prophet and witness of the Holy Spirit in the Church for the world. His experience of the Spirit does not lie outside the Church's common experience of Pentecost which is permanant in the Eucharist, that is to say of the unceasing breath and outpouring of the pentecostal gifts into the Church throughout all ages and in God's today.

There is no other means of discerning the work of the Spirit save in the conversion of hearts. In the ecclesial community as in the human heart, it is the Holy Spirit himself who prays, who invokes the blessed Name of Jesus in the depths of our hearts. The following text from the great Syrian master, Isaac of Nineveh, truly applies to St Seraphim, bearer of the Holy Spirit:

When the Spirit makes his abode in a man, he is no longer able to stop praying, because the Spirit never ceases to pray in him. Whether he sleeps or wakes, prayer is never separated from his soul. When he is eating, drinking, lying down, occupied in working, plunged in sleep, the perfume of prayer rises freely from his soul. From then on he does not order his prayer at set times, but prays all the time.[1]

This experience of the continuous prayer of the Spirit himself in our hearts echoes the saying of the Apostle Paul who speaks of the Spirit praying for us with sighs too deep for words (Rom. 6. 26 and Gal. 4. 6).

We find the same teaching on St Seraphim's lips:

When the Lord God, the Holy Spirit, visits us [he says] and comes to us in the fullness of his ineffable goodness, then we have to stop praying and refrain from prayer itself. The praying soul speaks and offers up words, but at the descent of the Holy Spirit it must be utterly silent so that it can clearly hear and truly understand the words of eternal life which the Spirit condescends to bring to it.

This attention centred on the experience and theology of the Holy Spirit which is inherent in eastern monasticism makes St Seraphim one with spiritual masters like St Symeon the New Theologian (eleventh century), St Tikhon of Zadonsk (eighteenth century), prophet of joy and hope in the kingdom of Christ, or Staretz Silouan of Mount Athos (†1938), whose writings bear abundant, unrivalled witness to the vivifying experience of the Holy Spirit.

Thus Orthodox tradition holds this sense of the actual, continuous presence of the Spirit of Pentecost in the hearts of Christians who are transformed and enkindled day by day in their hidden, interior life through the light, joy, peace, and love of the Holy Spirit. As long as the Church exists her Lord will stir up the manifold gifts of healing, exorcism, prophecy, judgement, tongues, discernment of spirits, compassion, and endurance.

'Learn to be peaceful,' said St Seraphim, 'and thousands around you will find salvation.'

The secret of this contagious influence and the light breeze of the coming of God's peace are revealed only to those men of the Spirit who from generation to generation constitute the heart of the community, of a rediscovered inward integrity, of humanity regenerate in Christ. These men as pillars of prayer uphold the entire world and preserve it from the destructive hate of the powers of evil.

What a prominent place and what a tragic realism these powers of evil occupy in the Staretz' spiritual vision! Though they do not readily reveal themselves in our everyday surroundings, Christ's advent into the world, that is, his taking up his abode in the human heart, forces the satanic powers to come out of the shadow. Those who, following in Christ's footsteps, have entered into the 'invisible warfare' know the power of the 'prince of this world' and the depths of his destructive hate. When a visitor asked the Staretz about demons he simply replied, 'They are hideous. Just as sinners cannot bear the brightness of angels, even so are evil spirits terrible to see.'

Here we are looking down into those dark, cold, infernal depths into which the saints are called to descend, conforming to the last degree of their divine Master's descent into hell.

This familiarity with evil and its dominion seems to be in sharp contrast to the traditional picture of the Staretz radiating gentleness and illuminating all things with the light of his paschal joy.

Yet St Seraphim's spiritual warfare just as much as his charismatic shining places him in the most authentic tradition of eastern monasticism, linked to the spirituality of the *Philokalia* from Mount Athos and the practice of the Jesus Prayer through the great staretz of Moldavia, Paissy Velitchkovsky. Through the work and influence of his disciples the tradition continues and spreads, and the monasteries of Optino and Sarov were for a long time spiritual centres for the Russian people. *The Way of a Pilgrim*[2] bears witness to the growth and power of this tradition in the nineteenth century beyond the walls of monasteries.

If it is true that no single saint fully expresses the spirituality of the Church in which he is rooted and to which he bears witness, we may yet say of St Seraphim that he undoubtedly surpassed to an exceptional degree the particular mode and type of monastic holiness from which he sprang. 'It seems', wrote Paul Evdokimov, 'that when he acquired the Holy Spirit he transcended monasticism itself.'

Although he left the world and chose the hard way of solitude and of a recluse for many years, this was only to come back to men at the end of his life, to find them again in their sickness of body and soul and to engender them to new life in the Holy Spirit. When he forsook the extreme forms of hermit life and returned to the world he may be said to have passed beyond institutional monasticism into the Holy Spirit. 'The fact that I am a monk and you a layman', he said to his disciple Motovilov in his catechism on the Holy Spirit, 'is something that we don't need to consider. . . . The Lord hears the prayers of a simple layman just as he does a monk's, provided they are both living in true faith and loving God from the depths of their heart.'

This is Staretz Seraphim's supreme message to the people of our day. When they offer God their hearts the Spirit is shown forth.

Man is then brought into the stream and certainty of the eternal life of the Holy Trinity. His whole life becomes light and communicates the risen Christ.


NOTES
[1] Isaac of Nineveh, *Treatises*.
[2] S.P.C.K. 1972, tr. R. M. French.

# Author's Introduction

'Towards the ending of history, rays appear on the summits of the Church; hardly discernible at first, they belong to the Day without Ending, the Day of the Age to come', writes Father Paul Florensky.[1] At the centre of this bright light shines forth the image of the holy Staretz, Seraphim of Sarov.

Seraphim of Sarov illumined the Church at the time when dark shades of secularization were beginning to threaten the country of Russia. In 1666 a decree was passed giving the state primacy of power over the authority of the Church. In 1721 Peter the Great abolished the Patriarchate, replacing it by a collegial organism, the Holy Synod, together with a procurator general as representative of the monarch. Peter's hostility to monasticism, guardian of ancient traditions, found expression in the closing of many monasteries. During the reign of Catherine II, who pursued the same politics as Peter, of 954 monasteries still in existence at this period 754 were closed and a decree was issued forbidding the opening of new ones without government permission. Representatives of the clergy and episcopate who raised their voices in defence of the Church's liberty often finished their life in prison or exile.[2]

This period of Russian history may be considered a prelude to the events that overtook that country after 1917. And it is in this historical context that the figure of Staretz Seraphim is to be seen.

His life (1759–1833) spans a period of six reigning sovereigns, from Elizabeth, daughter of Peter the Great, to Nicholas I. Each of those reigns introduced its own political and cultural changes into the country, so Seraphim is a witness of the military glory of Russia as well as of her distress and sorrows, of the time of slavery and the number-less abuses of the state's authority, of political conspiracies[3] and of peasants' riots and rebellions.

The eighteenth century, called the century of enlighten-ment, marks the beginning of an era when western ration-alistic ideas inundated the minds of the Russians. At first it was the upper intellectual classes of Russian society and young university students who were captivated by the inrush of the new ideas, but gradually materialistic propa-ganda succeeded in influencing the masses. With his penetrating prophetic mind the holy Staretz Seraphim clearly understood the impending danger of such a situation and it caused him to say: 'In our days . . . we are com-pletely estranged from life in Christ. We have lost the simplicity of the early Christians and with our so-called enlightenment we plunge ourselves into dark ignorance. . . .'

However, despite the prevalent dimming of faith and the measures of secularization decreed by the state, the synodical period of the Russian Church cannot be regarded merely as a time of decline. For a real revival of its spiritual forces is to be observed in the second half of the eigh-teenth century, and one that was particularly manifest in Russian monasticism. To a large extent this revival origin-ated from Mount Athos, which was regarded by the Rus-sians as the cradle of traditional Orthodoxy. A contemporary of Seraphim may be mentioned, a student of the theological academy of Kiev, Paissy Velitchkovsky (1722–1794), who went to Mount Athos, became a monk and there started his work of translating ancient Greek manuscripts on the practice of continuous prayer, known in Orthodoxy as the Jesus Prayer, or Prayer of the Heart. Paissy made a Slavonic translation of the *Philokalia*[4] containing extracts from the writings of the eastern fathers on prayer, pub-lished in 1793 and later translated into Russian. After his return from Mount Athos Paissy lived in the monastery of Niamets in Romania and from there inspired his disciples in Russia.

Another of St Seraphim's contemporaries, of the same spiritual family as Paissy, is Tikhon of Zadonsk, bishop of Voronezh (1724–1782), canonized by the Church. Like St Seraphim he experienced spiritual phenomena such as visions of the divine Light, and he spoke in his writings of the transfigurating power of the resurrection acting through the Holy Spirit in human nature and in the whole world. We may recognize an affinity with St Seraphim in this spiritual outlook and see Tikhon as his predecessor. Tikhon abandoned his episcopal throne and retired to the remote monastery of Zadonsk where he worked on translating the New Testament and psalms into Russian, and wrote letters to his spiritual children, as well as various articles which became very popular in Russia. Like Staretz Seraphim, both Paissy and Tikhon, while not belonging to any particular theological school, were true spiritual teachers living under the inspiration of the Holy Spirit.

It is difficult to fit the spiritual image of St Seraphim into an ordinary frame and to measure him according to normal standards. Liturgical chant praises him as 'an earthly angel and a heavenly man'. But from the psychological standpoint his personality though deeply rooted in old traditions yet bears marks of his epoch and environment. Like the man in the parable (Matt. 13.52) instructed in the mysteries of the kingdom of heaven, Staretz Seraphim brings forth out of his treasure things new and old. Not only is the wisdom of the ancient visionaries (Moses, Isaiah, Ezekiel) apparent in him, and an evangelical simplicity, but also the spiritual experience of the fathers of the Church and features of Russian saints such as St Sergius of Radonezh and St Nilus of Sora, together with his own experience of spiritual realities. He is above all a man of prayer and, while remaining loyal to the Church, at the same time through his own personal gifts he brings forth a new vision of monasticism which is more open to the world, more joyful and accessible.

Recognized by the people as a spiritual leader, he is one of those holy men called elders (startzi) by Orthodox people. In spite of his love for silence and solitude he would daily receive a multitude of people, greeting everybody with the paschal words: 'Christ is risen.' The Lord's resurrection filled his heart and mind with unceasing love, illuminating him with the radiance of divine grace.

The Russian philosopher Ivan Kireyevsky (1823–1886), whose wife Natalie had been one of St Seraphim's spiritual daughters and to whom he owed his return to Orthodoxy, wrote: 'There is one thing more important than all possible books and ideas—to find an Orthodox staretz before whom you can lay each of your thoughts and from whom you can hear not your own opinion but the judgment of the Holy Fathers. God be praised, such startzi have not yet disappeared in Russia.'[5]

## NOTES

[1] P. Florensky, *The Pillar and Foundation of Truth* (Berlin 1929), p. 125 (in Russian).

[2] One of the bishops struggling against Catherine's politics was Arseny Matsievitch, Metropolitan of Rostov, starved to death in 1771.

[3] Such as the assassinations of the Tsars Peter III and Paul, and the Decembrists' uprising in 1825.

[4] *Writings from the Philokalia on Prayer of the Heart* and *Early Fathers from the Philokalia* tr. Kadloubovsky and Palmer (Faber & Faber 1951 and 1954) give selections.

[5] Timothy Ware, *The Orthodox Church* (Penguin 1963), p. 133.

# 1

# From Childhood to the Priesthood

## CHILDHOOD

St Seraphim's biographers set the date of his birth at 19 July 1759 and place it in the town of Kursk. At his baptism he was given the name of Prokhor, which is that of the disciple of St John the Evangelist. To this disciple the beloved Apostle of Jesus Christ dictated his Apocalypse on the island of Patmos. Prokhor was the third child in the Moshnin family, the older children being a boy and a girl. Their father, Isidore, a stonemason and brickmaker, had several building yards in Kursk. He had nearly finished building a church with two altars (one consecrated to the Mother of the Lord and the other to St Sergius of Radonezh) when, in 1760, death took him away. His wife, Agatha, known and respected by her neighbours for her goodness and for her loving care for the sick, orphans, and widows, was a valiant woman and she took over the supervision of her husband's workshops. She often brought her younger son with her. One day, when they had climbed some scaffolding, Prokhor, a lively child, slipped and fell over the edge; fortunately he was unhurt. A 'fool'[1] in the town who witnessed the accident remarked at the time that the child must surely be 'one of God's elect'.

When Prokhor was ten years old a severe illness interrupted his education. One sleepless night the boy told his mother who was at his bedside that he had seen a vision of the Mother of God and that she had promised to heal him. In fact, a few days later when a procession with an icon of the Holy Virgin went past the Moshnins' house, Agatha carried her son to the icon, and very soon after this

1

Prokhor was well. The child resumed his lessons, and the
Bible and the lives of the saints became his favourite reading; in addition, he derived nothing but good examples
from his mother's hard-working life and the traditional
customs of his surroundings. The child also inherited from
his mother that love for his neighbour which he later
revealed when besieged by crowds on all sides. In this calm
and peaceful milieu he absorbed those wise and simple
counsels which he in turn was to give in later years:
'When you get up in the morning, after you've prayed,
give your room a thorough sweep and be sure to have a
good broom at hand.' Or again: 'Boil up your water
morning and evening, for hot water purifies both
body and soul.' 'Whatever you do, do it gently and
unhurriedly, because virtue is not a pear to be eaten in one
bite.'

Kursk, in spite of its eventful and tragic past,[2] was in
Prokhor's days an attractive town with its houses of red
and white limewashed brick, set in gardens. During Prokhor's life there were about twenty churches. The Moshnins lived in an old house near a church to which Prokhor
would go as often as he could; he sometimes met there
that fool in Christ who had foretold his destiny. The
influence of this fool, whose name we do not know, left its
mark on the child who always retained a great respect for
this type of holiness. However, he would never advise
anyone to adopt that kind of asceticism without being
quite sure that it was his or her true vocation. Seraphim
said that this way was not for the weak but only for someone with a strong body and a very sane spirit.

When Prokhor was seventeen his mother and his brother
Alexis decided that he should enter his elder brother's
trade. Having no liking for this kind of work, Prokhor
sought to transfigure the material concerns which oppressed him and to give them a spiritual significance. His
knowledge of the Gospels with his understanding of
Christ's parables led him to discern eternal truths within

2

earthly realities: buying and selling, loans, and capital became spiritual symbols to him.[3]

In later years, remembering the time he had spent in his brother's shop, St Seraphim said: 'A tradesman relies not so much on his goods as on the profit he derives from them; so the Christian should regard his virtues and good works not as ends in themselves but simply as means for attaining to the one thing necessary, the grace of the Holy Spirit.'

On days off Prokhor used to entertain his friends, Kursk tradesmen's sons, five of whom later entered the monastic life. During the long winter evenings they used to read the scriptures together, and the works of the Syrian, Egyptian, and Palestinian fathers who had left the world to live in the solitary places of those lands. Boundless space and vast horizons had always appealed to the Russians, and nothing held a stronger attraction for them than the concept of the desert which they extolled in their songs and poems. There were not, of course, in that Russian 'desert', those seas of sand and those rocky, arid mountains, but a desert of endless forests where the hermits had found a way of creating their own 'Thebaid'.[4]

Kursk also had its hermitage, founded on the spot where, in 1295, the icon of the Mother of God bearing Christ-Emmanuel on her heart was found at the foot of a tree. This was the icon before which the child Prokhor was healed; it was called the icon of the Sign (*Zaamenie*) or Apparition. In summer it was kept at the hermitage, known as the Hermitage of the Root (*Korennaya*) and in winter it was brought to Kursk.[5] However, the hermitage was a place of pilgrimage rather than a monastic centre, and the other monasteries in Kursk numbered very few members owing to the state's anti-monastic policy.[6] Most of those who did aspire to the monastic life went elsewhere.

About 300 kilometres away, on the borders of Tambov and Nijni-Novgorod, in the dense forest of Sarov, there lay a large monastery which had gathered within its walls many young men from Kursk, particularly from the merchant class. Prokhor had friends among them, and an inward call was drawing him to spend his novitiate there. However, before making a final decision he resolved to go on pilgrimage, with several companions, to the Monastery of the Caves at Kiev, the cradle of Russian monasticism. They intended to pray before the relics of the first monks, Anthony and Theodosius (the latter came from Kursk), and would seek the advice of a monk experienced in the guidance of souls. Since Kiev lay 450 kilometres away from Kursk, the boys had to make a long journey on foot before they could reach that ancient city called 'the mother of all Russian cities'.

After making his Communion and visiting the caves, Prokhor went to see a staretz who told him, as soon as he saw him coming: 'You will go to Sarov, my child, and your earthly pilgrimage will end there.' Then he added: 'The Holy Spirit will guide you in the Life and will make you his dwelling-place.' Prokhor was overcome with gladness when he knew that it was not just his own will that was guiding him to Sarov. He returned home full of hope.

After yielding up his share of his inheritance in favour of his brother, he said goodbye to his mother who, as a token of blessing, put a large brass cross round his neck, a family heirloom which Prokhor was to wear on his breast all his life. Then he took the road for Sarov, with two friends who had been his fellow-pilgrims to Kiev.

## THE HISTORY OF THE MONASTERY OF SAROV

What of this monastery of Sarov?

Situated on a hill and surrounded by dense forest, the solitude of Sarov had once been a fortress, built in a wild and beautiful place. In 1298, during the Tartar invasions, the fortress was taken by the enemy and made into the prince's residence. Bloody battles between the Russians and Tartars often raged there, and this has been confirmed by excavations which have brought to light armour and human bones. The Tartars occupied the district for about one hundred years and then, when they were defeated, the fortress was destroyed and left desolate. A forest grew over the site and only the name of the place, which the local inhabitants used to call 'the old fort' recalled its past.[7] For three hundred years 'the old fort' lay desolate, until in 1654 a monk called Theodosius came there; he built a hut and began to preach the Gospel in the neighbouring villages. A rumour spread of strange happenings at the fort: more than once a brilliant light lit up the whole hill and a sound like the peal of bells was heard in the surrounding district. This was a presage of the extraordinary events that were going to take place in those parts. They even dug up the ground in the belief that treasure was buried there, but burial crosses were all they found.

After the death of Theodosius another monk, John, came to dwell in a cave where he led a life of austerity and prayer. A community gathered round him and a church was built, and so new life came to the old fort. The community grew and became known by the villagers. Father John's rule was simple and austere, the monks living in poverty and gaining their bread by the work of their hands. Father John also undertook mission-work among the neighbouring peasants, many of whom were 'old believers'.[8] Unfortunately, relations with them were considered suspect, and as the result of an accusation, John was convicted, deported, and died as a prisoner in St Petersburg in 1737. His successor, Father Ephraim, was also deported and imprisoned in a fortress for sixteen years. When towards the end of his life he returned to his monastery, through the intervention of the clergy, he spent his remaining days attending to the needs of the afflicted.[9] His works of charity and his holiness drew many people to Sarov so that it soon became a place of pilgrimage. It needs to be said that the state's secularizing policy increased the people's spiritual thirst so that they were seeking guidance for their inner life. Thus this period marked the beginning of the renewal of the ancient tradition of startzi, men of God who were experienced ascetics possessing the gift of discernment of spirits.[10] Sarov had its own, such as Father Ephraim, a model of humility; Simon, a very virtuous man; Hieromonk (priest-monk) Joachim; Pakhomius; Nazarus.

## THE NOVITIATE
On the evening of 20 November 1778, Eve of the Feast of the Presentation in the Temple of the Virgin Mary, Prokhor crossed the threshold of the monastery of Sarov. Father Ephraim's successor, Abbot Pakhomius who came from Kursk, greeted him warmly and committed his spiritual education to Father Joseph, a good and intelligent monk. Prokhor recognized some of his fellow-townsmen among the monks: Alexander and Matthew; Hieromonk Joachim who refused a bishopric and an American mission in order to become librarian at Sarov and to share his knowledge with his brethren; Mark the hermit who withdrew to a cave in the forest in order to lead an ascetic life of prayer. According to the memoirs of his contemporaries, Prokhor was a strong, well-built young man with a lively intelligent expression and blue eyes reflecting his joyous spirit. Initiated into monastic rule, obedience, humility, and 'prayer of the heart', Prokhor was given various tasks. As baker he prepared the *prosfori* or loaves used for the divine liturgy; he was then apprenticed as carpenter and wood-worker and made burial crosses, rosaries and pectoral crosses. With his skilled fingers he was called 'Prokhor the carpenter'. He did all this work patiently without ever losing his peace. 'Nothing is better than obedience,' he was to say in later years. 'Oh, if only you had seen how happy I was in those days! Sometimes the monks who sang with me in choir came back from their work so tired that they hadn't the energy to sing. So I used to encourage them by

saying something to cheer them up, and then they would forget their weariness and the chant would go well. For, you see, the Lord wants people to be happy with him; and to say an encouraging word, even if it's in church, can hardly be a sin.' He combined the continuous Jesus Prayer[11] with his work. He said to the novices later: 'The whole art is there. Coming or going, sitting or standing, working or in church, let this prayer be ever escaping from your lips: "Lord, Jesus Christ have mercy on me a sinner!" With this prayer in your heart you will find inward peace and sobriety of body and soul.' And again, 'When you begin this invocation gather all the inner powers of your spirit and join them to those of your heart, and remain attentive. For one or two days, or longer, think only of the meaning of what you are saying, pronouncing each word attentively and separately. When the Lord warms your heart through grace and unites your powers into a simple, unified spirit, then inward prayer will become like a spring of living water that flows unceasingly, constantly nourishing and quickening you.'

These counsels were not mere book-learning; they were the fruit of personal experience, the crowning of his own endeavour but, still more, they came from the grace of the Holy Spirit.

Prokhor's superiors, noticing the patience, endurance and zeal with which he attended the liturgical services, made him a reader. From thenceforth he was always in church morning and evening, the first to arrive and the last to leave. At the same time he endeavoured to learn yet more, studying St Basil's *Hexameron*, St. Macarius' *Discourses*, St John Climacus' *Ladder of Divine Ascent*, and various extracts from the ascetic masters which the monks used to copy out themselves before the *Philokalia* was published, in spite of Peter the Great's decree forbidding monks to have ink in their cells. But, above all, Prokhor drank from the source of knowledge, the Bible itself. He used to call that 'the provisioning of the soul'. It was his custom to read standing before the icons. Thus he trained himself for the monastic and priestly life, and these biblical and patristic sources can always be recognized in the *Teaching* which he has left us. However, since he kept vigil late into the night and often abstained from all nourishment on fast days, he began to suffer from violent headaches. Later on he would never advise young monks to undertake severe mortifications: he would tell them to sleep for at least five or six hours and to rest again during the day: 'Because', he said, 'it is not the body that we should mortify but our passions. The body should be the soul's friend and helper in the work of perfection,[12] otherwise an exhausted body may have a weakening effect on the soul.' He was indeed speaking from experience because, four years after entering the monastery, he had to take to his bed, smitten with dropsy. Three years went by before his condition improved, in spite of such devoted care given him by Fathers Pakhomius and Joseph that St Seraphim said: 'Young novices need motherly care and affection more than parental authority.' One evening, thinking that death was near, Joseph assembled the brethren of the community for a vigil of prayer in the church and it was later learned, through Prokhor's guarded admission, that during the same night, as in his childhood, the Mother of God had appeared to him. Attended by the Apostles Peter and John she showed them the sick man and said: 'He is one of ours.' Then, coming up to Prokhor, she touched his hand and an ineffable well-being immediately spread through the invalid's whole body. The swelling from which he was suffering burst and a flow of water gushed out. Prokhor bore the scar to the end of his days. After his recovery it was decided to make a chapel of the cell where the holy Virgin had appeared to him and to add another room to serve as an infirmary. Prokhor was sent to collect funds in a number of towns, and he went to see his brother at Kursk; the latter gave him a large sum. On returning to Sarov he began building, and for a long time the cyprus-wood altar which he made for the chapel was kept as a memorial.

On 13 August 1786 Prokhor was at last permitted to make his monastic vows: from now on we shall know him by the name of Seraphim.[13]

## THE DEACON

In the following October Seraphim was ordained deacon; he remained as such for seven years, during which time he never missed a liturgical Office and expressed his grief at 'not being able to glorify God continuously as the angels do'. Later in confidence Father Seraphim disclosed some of the graces that he received at this period: like St Sergius of Radonezh he was privileged to see angels ministering at the altar with the priests and deacons, he heard them singing, and 'Nothing', he said, 'can be compared to this heavenly music. In my bliss which nothing could disturb I would forget everything. I wasn't conscious of being on earth; I only remembered coming into church and leaving it . . . but the time spent at the altar of the Lord was wholly light and splendour. My heart melted like wax in the heat of that ineffable joy.'

'One Holy Thursday,' he continues, 'I celebrated with Father Pakhomius. Before the "Entrance" with the Gospel, while the priest in the sanctuary was uttering the words: "Grant that the holy angels may enter with our entrance to minister with us and to glorify thy goodness," and while I was standing before the Royal Doors,[14] I was suddenly dazzled as though by a sunbeam and, as I glanced towards that light, I saw our Lord Jesus Christ in his aspect of Son of man, appearing in dazzling glory surrounded by the heavenly hosts, the seraphim and cherubim! He was walking through the air, coming from the west door towards the middle of the church. He stopped before the sanctuary, raised his arms and blessed the celebrants and people. Then, transfigured, he went into his icon by the Royal Door, still surrounded by the angelic escort which continued to illumine the church with its shining light. As for me, who am only dust and ashes, I was given the grace of receiving an individual blessing from the Lord so that my heart overflowed with joy.'[15]

In the words of those who witnessed the scene, the expression on the deacon Seraphim's face suddenly changed and instead of continuing with his ministry he stood rooted to the spot. Then two deacons took him by the arms and brought him into the sanctuary where he remained for two hours without being able to utter a word. His face changed from being white as snow to a flame colour that must have been lit up from within.

During this same period of his diaconate an event occurred of a kind that sometimes happens in the monastic life: it was during the famine of 1792. Short of bread, one night the monks held a vigil of prayer, and in the morning the deacon Seraphim was sent to the barns to collect what remained of the flour. To his amazement he found a barn full of all kinds of grain, wheat, rye and barley. From then onwards the monastery was never short of bread.

A VISIT TO DIVEYEVO: MOTHER ALEXANDRA
When Staretz Joseph died Father Pakhomius became spiritual guide to the deacon Seraphim. He celebrated the Offices daily and often took Seraphim with him on his pastoral visits in the neighbourhood. One day in early June 1789 their road took them through the village of Diveyevo, 12 kilometres from Sarov, where there was a small community of nuns. They learned that the foundress, Mother Alexandra, was seriously ill. She was well known to the monastery of Sarov and to the neighbouring peasants for her intelligence, valour, humility, and compassion. After the death of her husband and only daughter she took the veil at Kiev and sold her large estates. The Mother of God, she said, then guided her to the village of Diveyevo, which was an industrial centre, its population working in the iron mines. There, with the blessing of Father Ephraim of

Sarov, she carried out a great ministry in succouring people in their affliction, caring for the women and children exhausted by their work, mothering the orphans and counselling peasants from the surrounding villages. She had a church built at Diveyevo and gathered round her several women and girls who wanted to live a life of prayer: this was the beginning of that community to which Father Pakhomius gave the same rules as were observed at Sarov. It became a kind of daughter-house to the monastery, the nuns being responsible for looking after the fathers' linen and clothing, and receiving food and fuel in return.

Then, in the month of June 1789, Father Pakhomius found Mother Alexandra on her death-bed. He gave her the holy sacraments and received from her the sum of forty thousand rubles for the upkeep of the little community. She begged him never to forsake it. Father Pakhomius gave her his promise and told her that after his death the deacon Seraphim would be responsible for it. Reassured by these promises, Mother Alexandra bade her farewells and died on 13 June.

That was a providential visit, for, when the time came, Father Seraphim consecrated all his powers and spiritual gifts to this community.

## THE PRIEST

Four years later, on 2 September 1793, the deacon Seraphim, then aged thirty, received priestly ordination and became a Hieromonk. From then on he celebrated the liturgy daily. It was for him, as he said, 'A well of water springing up into everlasting life.'

All his life the grace of the priesthood gave him the power to develop those graces which Christ bequeathed to his apostles: healing diseases, freeing the possessed, preaching the Word of God. Information about his ministrations is not found in the latter part of his life, but there is a note in the archives that Seraphim always wore the tokens of the priesthood[16] when he received Communion and when he absolved penitents. He always urged the faithful to frequent Communion and advised priests to facilitate this, 'because', he added, 'it gives the recipient so great a grace: a man may be the worst of sinners, but if he comes to his Lord with humility and contrition he is completely purified and renewed'. His mysterious words spoken on another occasion have also been preserved, when he was consoling a widow whose husband had died without receiving the sacraments: 'My joy, have no fear of his not being saved, for it sometimes happens that someone who has been prevented from making his Communion through unavoidable circumstances may receive the true benefit of the holy Mysteries donated invisibly by the angel of the Lord.'[17]

Abbot Pakhomius died on 6 November 1794. In him Father Seraphim lost another staretz and the spiritual help which he still needed. 'Joseph and Pakhomius were', in his own words, 'two pillars of fire with their flames leaping up to heaven.' He asked permission of Pakhomius' successor, Father Isaac, to go and live as a hermit in the forest; the permission was granted. Seraphim was earnestly seeking for prayer and the increasing pilgrimages to the monastery were a hindrance to the life of silence which he loved. He wanted to maintain in its integral purity that way of a monk which has always been regarded by the Church as akin to the life of the angels.[18] Moreover, his reply to his brethren when they reproached him for wanting to 'leave' them was: 'It's not because I don't love my brethren that I'm going away, but because we have received the angelic seal and nothing impure must stain it.' He was given a permit which he had to renew each year because hermitages, like the monasteries, were under government surveillance. The document stated that Hieromonk Seraphim had gone to live in a remote house belonging to the monastery because his state of health made community life difficult for him.

Thus on 21 November 1794, the actual anniversary of

his arrival at the monastery, Father Seraphim left it to go and 'rest', as the wording on his permit put it. He attained the solitude of the forest.

## NOTES

[1] In Russia 'simples' or 'fools in Christ' were regarded as blessed, as those 'poor in spirit' of the Beatitudes. Most of them were far from being mentally deficient or idiots: by voluntarily adopting a repulsive appearance they concealed their charismatic gifts which would otherwise have attracted admiring throngs.

[2] This fortified town dates from the ninth century and takes its name from the river Kur which flows through it. Down the centuries it was several times razed to the ground by the Tartars and always rebuilt again.

[3] We find the idea of the transfiguration of the world from within in the works of Prokhor's contemporary, Bishop Tychon of Zadonsk, whose book, *Spiritual Treasures Garnered in the World*, was well known in Russia.

[4] Monasteries founded in places where anchorites had previously lived. They also came to be called 'solitude' or 'desert' (*Pustina*).

[5] After the 1917 revolution the icon was taken out of the country by the emigrants and is now in America. It is brought to Europe from time to time and the Orthodox churches in France have received it several times.

[6] After Peter the Great's reforms, of the four monasteries in existence in Kursk before his reign only one remained, and monastic profession became rarer and rarer.

[7] There is a description in the old archives of Sarov: 'It is a great forest of oaks, firs and spruce, inhabited by wild animals, bears, lynx, moose, martens, beavers, otters and others, living along the banks of the rivers Satis and Sarovka. These places are uninhabitable; men come there only occasionally, to take the honey.'

[8] After the church reforms at the end of the seventeenth century, a large number of the faithful separated from the official church and, fleeing from government persecutions, sought refuge in the forests where they organized themselves into small communities.

[9] There was a famine in 1775, due to the uprising of the Cossack Pugatchev who stirred up the peasants and posed as Tsar Peter III, husband of Catharine II, assassinated at court; the abbot Ephraim then opened the monastery's granaries and distributed corn to the neighbouring people.

10 Orthodox monasticism is not organized into congregations and orders as in the west; it is orientated towards the practice of asceticism in accordance with the Rule drawn up by St Basil of Cappadocia (325–375), the founder of cenobitism. The monks' life, consecrated to prayer and work, is directed by a superior called *higoumen* or *archimandrite*. But alongside this official direction the monks may choose a brother experienced in the guidance of souls from among themselves (a staretz).

11 The repeated invocation of the Name of Jesus, accompanied by metanies, tends to create a perfect union of body and spirit which prepares the monk for becoming the instrument of the Holy Spirit. Cf. 'The Prayer of Jesus' by Francois Neyt in *Sobornost* No. 9, Summer 1974, pp. 641 ff.

12 The Orthodox quest for perfection, based on Matt. 5.48, has nothing in common with that 'perfectionism' which is sometimes encountered in the west and regarded with such mistrust.

13 The name Seraphim suggests a shining, light-filling being. Translated from the Hebrew this name means 'flaming' and bears within it the reflection of those lights and flames with which the heavenly spirits encircle the world and the throne of God.

14 The Royal Doors form the central doorway in the *iconostsis* or screen separating the sanctuary from the body of the church.

15 'When Christ is present at the eucharistic table, this festal table grows and bears us to the very heart of God's hospitality, into the circle of love and life.' B. Bobrinskoy: '*Présence réelle et communion eucharistique*' in *le Revue des sciences philosophiques et theologiques*, 1964, p. 4.

16 These consist of stole, cuffs and pectoral cross.

17 Here again we see a reference to the invisible ministry of angels during the divine liturgy.

18 Cf. Louis Bouyer, *The Meaning of the Monastic Life*, which gives a theological exposition of the 'angelic life' of the monk. London, Burns & Oates 1955 (translation).

# 2

# The Ascetic Way:
# the Call of the Desert

## THE HERMITAGE

Ever since his novitiate Father Seraphim had felt called
by the desert. Sometimes he used to go away into retreat
and had even built a little hut on a wooded hill overlooking
the river Sarovka, about 5 kilometres from the monastery.
He planted a vegetable garden and returned from time to
time to stay there. He consecrated this hermitage to the
Virgin of Tenderness whose icon he had placed in his cell.[1]

When he began his life as a solitary Father Seraphim was
not yet forty years old, but he seemed prematurely aged.
That was, in fact, one of the reasons why he had so easily
obtained permission to leave the monastery. He was weak-
ened [by sickness and fasting, and his legs were swollen
and covered with sores.

He was, moreover, not the only one to be living the
hermit life in that vast forest; halfway between the monastery and his retreat some other monks had found a
refuge where they could live apart from the daily clamour.
There were Mark the hermit, Hieromonk Dorotheus,
Hierodeacon Alexander and the monk Matthew, all from
Kursk, and they sometimes came to see Father Seraphim.
All that region, rather rocky, hollowed with caves, inter-
sected with valleys, wooded with ancient firs, spruce, and
gigantic oaks, offered an ideal spot for a monk in quest of
peace and quiet. From the very beginning of his solitude
Father Seraphim set out to make his desert a Holy Land.
He had always been impressed by the reports of those who
had gone on pilgrimage to the Lord's country, not least

by what he heard from Hieromonk Meletius who had just returned to the monastery after a year in Palestine.[2] All this would supplement his daily reading of the Gospels. He was never separated from these and used to take them with him everywhere in his wallet. 'I never let a single day go by without this reading,' he confessed, 'because not only is my soul gladdened by the Divine Word, but even my body is refreshed by it. It's like talking with the Lord when I call to mind his life and passion. Night and day I ascribe glory to him, worship him, and thank him for his goodness.'

So in his desert he chose places which reminded him of events in the life of our Lord and of his holy Mother. For instance, he would go and sing the Virgin's hymns and re-read the story of the annunciation in a place which he called Nazareth; in a cave which he called Bethlehem he extolled the incarnation of God made Man. He also had his mountain of the Beatitudes, his Mount Tabor and his Gethsemane. As for the joy of Easter, he relived it every day, constantly singing the hymns of the resurrection. Thus, far-away Palestine came very near and he lived at Jesus' feet as though in the Holy Land, 'watching in the interior Jerusalem of his heart', ceaselessly keeping the Name of Jesus on his lips.

His days were spent in various tasks: he dug the ground, erected a fence to protect his dwelling from the incursion of wild animals, prepared the ingredients for his stew-pan (for he lived on his own produce). He brought only a little bread from the monastery to last the whole week and it was known that he shared this with the animals in the forest. He was seen in the company of a huge bear who, meek as a lamb, took its food from his hand. He used to sing while he worked, and one of the songs he loved was about the glory of the Mother of God, patron of the hermitage. Sometimes while he worked his soul would become rapt in prayer, absorbed in God. Then, without being aware of it, his hands would let go of the spade or axe and, eyes shut, he would be lost to the world. People seeing him in this

16

state would quietly steal away or else wait for his rapture to end, and it sometimes lasted for more than an hour.

On the eve of Sundays and festivals he usually returned to the monastery to assist at Vespers and Matins and to make his Communion on the following day. On these occasions the monks, his brethren, welcomed him joyfully and gathered round to hear him speak.

'If you would order the inner dwelling-place of your soul,' he told them, 'first of all prepare the necessary material so that the heavenly architect can begin the building. The house must be light and airy, with windows, which are the five senses, so that the light of heaven, the sun of righteousness, can penetrate to our inner dwelling. The door of the house is Christ in person, for he said, "I am the door." He both guards the house and lives in it. Yes, if your soul is so prepared, God can come in and dwell there.'

He also said: 'When mind and heart are united in prayer, without any distraction, you feel that spiritual warmth which comes from Christ and fills the whole inner being with joy and peace.'

'We have to withdraw from the visible world so that the light of Christ can come down into our heart. Closing our eyes, concentrating our attention on Christ, we must try to unite the mind with the heart and, from the depths of our whole being, we must call on the Name of our Lord, saying: "Lord, Jesus Christ, have mercy on me a sinner." '

'To the degree that love for the Lord warms the human heart, one finds in the Name of Jesus a sweetness that is the source of abiding peace.'

When evening fell the monks would go to Compline and Father Seraphim went back to his hermitage, bringing his rations for the week. His return was eagerly awaited by the inhabitants of the forest. Birds, animals, and reptiles came up to his door and the father fed them. One who witnessed this scene, the deacon Alexander, asked Father Seraphim one day how he managed to feed so many

17

creatures. 'I've no idea', he replied, 'but God knows. As for
me, I've always enough in my wallet.' The same deacon
Alexander saw a huge bear lying quietly at Father Seraphim's feet. This 'multiplication of loaves', it will be remembered, had happened before at the monastery in the
feeding of the hungry, and now it was happening again
on behalf of the animals and was expressive of Father
Seraphim's love for all God's creatures.

His hermit's cell was almost bare, without even a bed to
lie down on, for Seraphim slept on a sack of stones collected
from the banks of the Sarovka. He wore the same cassock
all the year round, a kind of white tunic girded with a
string; but in winter he wore a heavy greatcoat. A black
*calotte*[3] covered his head; he wore high boots in winter and
sandals plaited from birch-bark in summer.

Seraphim loved this poverty bordering on destitution.
Before long, in spite of his wanting to live hidden away, he
became more and more widely known. Several monks
asked to come and live with him in his hermitage; Seraphim raised no objection, but his visitors left him after only
a few days there, unable to endure such austerity. If it is
true that he had no real disciples at Sarov, the fact remains
that, as used to be said, all the monks were his disciples.

In 1796 Seraphim was offered the office of superior of a
neighbouring monastery, but in his humility he refused it.

An ever-increasing number of people, though, seeking
his spiritual advice, came to see him at his hermitage, not
content with meeting him on Sundays at the monastery.
These visits oppressed him, especially those of women. So
he went to ask counsel of Abbot Isaiah, who advised him to
free himself from them. Father Seraphim then asked God
for a 'sign' to resolve this problem, because he did not want
to be unloving in refusing to see women; he also appealed
to the Mother of God. Then, the day after Christmas, as he
was returning to his hill, he saw that the path leading to it
was blocked from both sides by great branches of fir trees
blown down by the wind. He understood the meaning of

this 'sign', blocked the path still further, and from then on
his solitude became even more austere. Even the monks
themselves used to visit him more rarely.

## CONFLICT WITH THE DEVIL

Several testimonies collected in the archives of Sarov
attempt to describe something of Father Seraphim's life
during the nights and days of his recluse period. We may
well call this time the hour of battle with the powers of
darkness. It sometimes seemed to Seraphim as though the
walls of his hut were collapsing or that raging foes were
assailing him from all sides, or that wild beasts were
pouncing on his hut; he heard howls and cries, and sometimes he even felt himself lifted up and then violently
flung to the ground.[4] Seraphim was asked if he had seen
demons. He was silent and then said simply, 'They are
despicable.'

After some time, the nature of the attacks changed:
heavy anxiety and anguish gripped the hermit's heart, deep
depression overwhelmed him, dark thoughts troubled his
spirit. Seraphim saw himself damned, abandoned by God,
and it was then that his agony approached despair. 'He who
has chosen the hermit life', he said later, 'must feel himself
constantly crucified. . . . The hermit, tempted by the spirit
of darkness, is like dead leaves chased by the wind, like
clouds driven by the storm; the demon of the desert bears
down on the hermit at about mid-day and sows restless
worries in him, and distressing desires as well. These temp-
tations can only be overcome by prayer.'

This spiritual battle must have gone on for years; it was
only at the end of his life that it became known, through
his guarded disclosures, that he had spent a thousand days
and a thousand nights in prayer, kneeling on a granite rock
or prostrate in his cell, overcoming satanic powers. He also
disclosed his fasting and penance. 'Do you know ground
elder?' he asked someone. 'Do you know how nourishing
it is? For three years I ate nothing else. I dried it for the

19

winter and it was a very good victual.' Since he had barricaded the path leading to his hermitage and no longer went to the monastery to fetch his ration no one knew how he managed to feed himself.

## IN THE HANDS OF BRIGANDS

To crown all, one day when Seraphim was chopping wood in the forest three men appeared and angrily demanded money. The rumour of treasure hidden in the forest spread among the simple folk and kindled their avarice. When the hermit replied that he had none they would not believe him. To extract it from him, they struck him, bound him with ropes, and hurled him to the ground, unconscious. Believing him to be dead, they went and searched his hut but found nothing save a few potatoes. The sack which they thought to be full of money contained only the stones which served him for a mattress. Panic-struck, the men fled. When Seraphim came to himself he summoned the strength to free himself from his bonds and to drag himself painfully to the monastery. Without saying what had happened to him, he simply asked to be taken to the infirmary. The doctor from the neighbouring town of Arzamas was sent for; he diagnosed fractures of the skull and ribs, and many other wounds. While remedies were being prepared Father Seraphim felt himself transported to another world. The Mother of God appeared to him again, still attended by the Apostles Peter and John, and she repeated the same words: 'He is one of ours.' The rapture lasted for four hours. Then the Father felt a great solace. However, his convalescence took several months; his hair turned white, and he remained a hunchback for the rest of his life.[5]

## RETURN TO THE HERMITAGE

When he returned to his desert, Seraphim could only walk leaning on his staff or on the handle of his axe, yet he did not lessen his gardening nor his work in the forest. A new

neighbour had settled not far from his hermitage: Hieromonk Nazarus who had previously been one of the editors
of the *Philokalia*.[6] When he returned to Sarov after a life
of active work he built himself a hermit's cell on the banks
of the Sarovka, where Father Seraphim met him. Nazarus
practised silence and the prayer of the heart; he used to
spend his nights psalmodizing and singing canticles under
the stars. Bears and other animals came to him fearlessly
and, like Seraphim, he used to feed them from his hand.
He died in 1809.

Another staretz, Hieromonk Isaiah, abbot of the monastery, resigned in 1805 and became a frequent visitor
to Father Seraphim's hermitage. Unable to traverse on foot
the 5 kilometres which separated the hermitage from the
monastery, he had himself driven to the recluse in a little
carriage; he would spend long hours with Seraphim, whom
he had chosen as his confessor. But these friendly visits
were brought to an end by his death.[7]

Seraphim then rose to a further degree of asceticism,
that of silence, which according to St Gregory of Nyssa
'gives access to contemplation of the invisible'. The monks
who have attained it were nearly all hermits, such as St
Macarius the Great, St Isaac of Syria, St John Climacus,
St Maximus the Confessor, and St Symeon the New
Theologian. Their writings were Father Seraphim's cease-
less nourishment and he discovered 'silence' in their school.
'No spiritual exercise', he said, 'can be compared with
silence. Though it is not just our tongue that we have to
restrain, but, even more, our spirit.' On the other hand:
'Anyone coming into the land of silence must always bear
in mind the end to which it gives access, so that his heart
may never stray.' He used to quote St Isaac of Syria's words:
'When the mouth and lips grow quiet, then the heart—
that chamberlain of the soul and mind—reigning over the
senses, and the spirit too—that swift bird—grow quiet, for
the Master of the house is there.'

Abbot Isaac's successor was Niphont, ninth superior of

the monastery of Sarov. In his eyes observance of the rule
was one of the most important obligations of monastic life.
Inevitably he found Father Seraphim's behaviour some-
what irregular because the hermit, striving to attain utter
peace of soul by means of total silence, no longer came to
the church. So questions were asked as to whether he was,
in fact, receiving Communion in his hermitage. The
superior summoned his council who decided to send an
ultimatum to Father Seraphim ordering him to come to
Communion on Sundays as before, and saying that if his
legs made the journey impossible then he must come back
permanently to the monastery. The monk who brought the
hermit his provisions for the week was to deliver this
decision of the council. The first time, Seraphim made no
reply, but the second time, when the monk left, the old
man rose and followed him without uttering a word. It was
8 May 1810. Fifteen years had elapsed since Father Seraphim had chosen the solitary life.

ENCLOSURE
On arrival at the monastery Seraphim went to the infirmary
to have the sores on his legs treated, then he went straight
to the church for the celebration of Vespers. On the following day he made his Communion, went to see the superior,
and then shut himself in his cell. It was understood that
he had enclosed himself. We have no details of this period
of his life any more than of the preceding one; we only
know that his cell-neighbour, Brother Paul, brought him
food and water—a little gruel and chopped cabbage. On
some days the recluse did not even open his door and then
the brother took the food away again. With the superior's
permission the Blessed Sacrament was brought to his cell.
At night he was to be seen taking a short walk round the
church or in the direction of the adjacent cemetery, but he
never went out by day.

One day, 15 August 1815, the Bishop of Tambov, after
celebrating the liturgy at the monastery, came and

knocked on Father Seraphim's door; he received no reply. Abbot Niphont, who was with him, fearing that the recluse might be dead, wanted to force the door, but the Bishop restrained him: 'If we do that we might do something displeasing to God.' But a week later, to the astonishment of all the monks, when a young couple arrived (the Governor of Tambov and his wife) Father Seraphim opened the door of his cell and gave them his blessing.

Had his time of enclosure come to an end? One thing is certain, that from then on, after those five years of claustration, Father Seraphim no longer kept his door shut. His voice was heard reciting the prayers and singing Matins and Compline; and if a number of monks gathered outside his door they often heard him reading and commenting on the Gospels. There were several monks who even saw him in his cell and talked with him, such as the monks Gabriel and George, and Hieromonks Abel and Sergius who fortunately made notes of these conversations.

On the other hand, since this was a time of frequent wars when many young men were asking to be received at the monastery for the sake of dodging recruitment, Father Seraphim made no bones about telling one or another of them what trials a monk must expect. He would say, for example: 'A monk is like a cloth that the fuller presses, beats, washes, and rinses to make it white as snow. In bearing humiliations, insults, and afflictions, a monk purifies his soul and becomes shining like silver refined in the fire.'

He also said: 'It's no good becoming a monk without trying to learn patience. The true mark of a monk is bearing wrongs patiently and meekly. Just as a soldier cannot go to war without arms, no more can a monk begin a life of prayer without arming himself with patience.'

And on the subject of prayer: 'External prayer is not enough, and monks who do not unite it with inner prayer are only a puff of smoke. A monk without inner prayer is like a fish out of water.' And again: 'A monk must not stop short at the first degrees of his endeavour; he must persevere and press on to higher degrees, for it is only when he reaches those that he can acquire the grace of the Holy Spirit.' He never advised young monks to adopt the solitary life but told them that attacks by the devil could best be resisted in community, while in solitude the powers of hell pounced on a hermit like lions.

Once Father Seraphim had opened his door visitors were never lacking, and it was not only young monks and novices who sought his counsel but superiors from neighbouring monasteries as well. The Father urged these latter to be kind and love their brethren, to have 'the love of a mother for her children', to bear patiently with their weaknesses and even with their diverse failings. He told them that this was what it cost to gain true inner peace. 'Learn to be peaceful', he would say, 'and thousands of souls around you will find salvation.'

When a visitor entered he would give him the kiss of peace and, if it were a priest or the superior of a monastery, he would prostrate himself before him. His little cell, lit by an oil lamp which burned before the icon of the Virgin of Tenderness, had hardly any daylight because the two small windows, looking on to a ravine, were almost entirely screened by bits of curtain or paper. A table and a log for Seraphim to sit on were all the furnishing. It was in this haven of poverty that the Father listened to souls and absolved sins.

He became a staretz whose renown was to spread abroad far beyond the walls of the monastery of Sarov.

NOTES

1 The Virgin Mary is represented at the moment of uttering her *Fiat*; with lowered eyes she is very humbly listening to the archangel's words. We know that Father Seraphim was never separated from this icon and that he died kneeling in prayer before it.

2 His memoirs were published in Moscow a few years later.

[3] monastic cap.

[4] Such manifestations are a frequent occurrence in the lives of ascetics past and present. In France, for instance, Seraphim's contemporary, the holy Curé d'Ars (1786–1859), experienced identical manifestations.

[5] The criminals were found; they were peasants from a neighbouring village. Father Seraphim would not have them arrested for trial. Fully repentant, they came and threw themselves at the old man's feet, imploring his forgiveness.

[6] Born near Sarov in 1735, he spent his novitiate in the monastery and was ordained hieromonk at the age of forty. His sermons attracted the attention of the ecclesiastical authorities and he was sent to Northern Russia to reorganize and renew the monastic life at the monastery of Valaamo. There he introduced the rule lived at Sarov and, under his direction, the community became a centre of spiritual enlightenment. He was then sent as a missionary to the Aleutian Islands and it was several years after this that Metropolitan Gabriel enlisted him for the work of editing the *Philokalia*.

[7] The monks' council asked Father Seraphim to succeed him but once again he refused. He said that to accept it one needed a special vocation which he did not feel he possessed.

# 3

# The Staretz of Sarov

## THE VOCATION OF STARETZ

After thirty-seven years of preparation Father Seraphim's true vocation now became manifest: that of staretz.[1] The years spent in the desert, the conflicts with the powers of hell, his silence and enclosure were only the prelude to this period when, at over sixty years of age, Seraphim came to devote himself to suffering humanity and to spend the rest of his life besieged by the crowds who came to him seeking his help and comfort.

At this troubled period the peasant class, crushed by poverty and servitude, came to the men of God for advice and consolation; while as for intellectuals, still full of the notions of eighteenth-century France, only a few of them found their way to the startzi's cells.

It is a fact that the Tsar Alexander I was one of those who used to visit startzi. In 1816 he became firm friends with one of Seraphim's admirers, Anthony, abbot of the monastery at Kiev, who, it is said, may have sent him to Seraphim. In any case it is not out of the question that it was under Seraphim's influence that Alexander abandoned the throne in 1825 and lived in Siberia until 1864 under the name of Staretz Fedor Kusmitch.

Much had taken place during Father Seraphim's time as a recluse. There had been wars and conquests, invasions and changes on the throne. Fifty-eight thousand Russians had fallen in Napoleon's campaign at Borodino; Moscow burned, taken by the enemy; then in 1813 the people celebrated the liberation of the country. All these events seemed to leave no mark on the Staretz' life, yet a number of soldiers have testified to the power of his prayers which saved them when they were in mortal danger. When they asked for these prayers, people sent him packets of candles. To those who were astonished at seeing his cell lit up by their flame the Staretz explained: 'It says in the Bible that God told Moses to light a fire of expiation in order to avert God's wrath from the people; since there are so many folk asking me to pray for them and I can't remember all their names, I'm burning a candle for each of them.'

Besides this, since Sarov lay near the highroad leading to the barracks at Arzamas, army units passed along it and sometimes a detachment would stop at the monastery where some of the soldiers would be received by the Staretz. 'We have sinned greatly,' he would say to them, 'and we must pray much and implore the Lord to be merciful.' He offered himself as a living prayer, and his cell, which he had not yet left, became as it were a spiritual battlefield where the Staretz snatched souls from Satan's grasp. 'All through these vigils', Father Seraphim later declared, 'I felt a pain in my body as though I were being burned.'

## MICHAEL MANTUROV

In 1822 a young man, Michael Manturov, was brought to Father Seraphim with diseased legs and hardly able to walk. He had been in government service in the Baltic States and had married there. When he fell ill he had to retire and come home to live on his estate which was about 40 kilometres from Sarov; he and his younger sister Helen had inherited this property from their grandfather. 'Why have you come to see me?' the Staretz asked him. Manturov explained about his illness and how the doctors had been unable to help him. 'Do you believe in God?' Father Seraphim then asked; and when the invalid replied in the affirmative he said: 'Well, my joy, if you believe in God, you must be confident that a believer is able to obtain all things from God through faith. So now, believe firmly that

God is able to heal you, and I, unworthy as I am, will go
and pray for you.' When he had said this he went to the
back of his cell and then returned with oil from the lamp
that was burning before the icon of the Virgin. He asked
the young man to uncover his legs, saying to him: 'By the
grace given me from the Lord, you are the first whom I
heal.' Then he took some pieces of blessed bread which he
used to dry for giving to visitors; he stuffed handfuls of
these into Manturov's pockets and told him to return to
the monastery guest house. The invalid, who normally
could hardly stand, hesitated for a moment; then, feeling
a strange power upholding him, he threw himself at the
Staretz' feet to thank him for his cure. Father Seraphim
raised him up saying, 'Is this healing Seraphim's doing?
No, no, my joy, only God does this, and you owe your cure
to him and to his holy Mother.'[2]

Some time after this, certain monks accused Father
Seraphim of anointing the sick without using either the
traditional Office of Holy Unction or the rite which follows
the blessing of oil on the eve of great feasts. The Staretz
simply replied: 'Do we not read in the Bible that the
apostles anointed the sick in the name of Christ and healed
them? So whom should we follow if not the apostles?'
Acting in this way, Father Seraphim obeyed Christ's com-
mandment: 'Go and heal the sick.'

## MANTUROV'S VOW

Not long after this, Manturov returned to Sarov to ask the
Staretz how he was to testify his gratitude to God for his
cure. Hardly had he reached the Staretz' cell before he was
met by the latter opening his door and saying to him:
'Well, my joy, haven't we promised the Lord to give
thanks?' Amazed that the Staretz had read his heart, Manturov asked what he was to do. Then, looking at Manturov
with profound love, Father Seraphim uttered these words:
'Well, my joy, if you can, give God all you possess.'
Momentarily taken aback, Manturov thought he had mis-

understood; he was silent, he hesitated. But the Staretz gave him no time to think and said immediately: 'Now let go of all worldly care: the Lord will never forsake you, neither here nor in the life to come, he will always give you your daily bread.' Ardent and impulsive, Manturov felt ready to obey this saint whom he already loved with all his heart. 'Tell me what I'm to do!' he said. 'All right, my joy,' answered the Staretz, 'we'll go and pray, to discover God's will. I'll send for you later,' and he sent him away. A few days later he sent to fetch him. Seraphim told Manturov that he was to sell his lands, free his serfs, and then buy forty acres of land at Diveyevo at the place which he would show him. 'God has predestined this land', he said, 'for the community of Diveyevo.' While Seraphim was speaking Manturov was thinking of his young wife whom he had just married, accustomed to the life of ease lived by the nobility of those days. Again a momentary hesitation stirred his heart but he quickly recovered himself and resolutely made the vow of poverty which the Staretz was asking of him.

However, his wife, indignant at her husband's decision, bombarded Manturov with reproaches, but he remained unmoved. He endured his wife's revilings with patience and good humour, and in the end she relented. When she became a widow she embraced the monastic life at Diveyevo, and she wrote in 1856: 'When my husband made a vow of poverty I never ceased to reproach him. The only answer he would give was a sigh, and this exasperated me yet more. At one time, in winter, so great was our poverty that we did not even have any oil for the lamp. The evenings were long and gloomy. I could bear it no longer and began weeping and complaining and blaming Father Seraphim for it. My husband still said nothing. Suddenly I heard a slight crackling coming from the direction of the icon. I looked up without being able to believe my eyes: our lamp, which a moment ago was empty, was filled to the brim with oil and was burning with a bright little light. Then I dissolved into tears and said again and again: "O holy Mother of God, for love of Christ, forgive me a miserable sinner." After that, in spite of all our ordeals, I never grumbled again. Even now, when I recall all this, I am overwhelmed.'

When he had disposed of all his wealth Michael Manturov came to live with his wife in a little house in Diveyevo village and put himself at Father Seraphim's disposal, awaiting directions from him. At that time the Staretz still did not leave his cell but received visitors at the monastery.

One day, in 1823, he sent for Manturov, bowed to him, and handed him a stake, telling him to plant it in a field behind the church at Diveyevo which Mother Alexandra had built. He indicated the number of paces to be made from the church's apse to the middle of the field. Manturov happily carried out the Staretz' direction. The following year, in 1824, Father Seraphim gave him four small stakes and told him to plant them round the first one to make a square. Intrigued, Manturov wondered what all this meant but did not dare ask for an explanation. Not long afterwards the mystery resolved itself when the owner of the field gave it to the community of Diveyevo as a gift, for them to build a mill there.

This event, insignificant in itself, bears witness to the gift of foretelling the future which was bestowed on Seraphim.

THE GIFT OF INSIGHT

This insight seemed quite natural to him because, as he said, it arose from some 'sign' received from God during prayer, it came in connection with those people who asked him about a decision to be made or the choice of a vocation. The father saw the future of those who questioned him outlined before him.

These predictions of the holy Staretz must have spread from one monastery to another and to the surrounding villages; the peasants even took him for a seer and came to consult him when in difficulty. Among other incidents, this is what the deacon Alexander recalls: 'One day when I came out of the church and went past Father Seraphim's cell a peasant, all out of breath, called out to me, "Are you Seraphim?" "No," I said, "but what do you want him for?" "I've been told he's a seer, and someone's stolen my horse, and without it I'm ruined, I and my family." At that moment I saw Father Seraphim in his doorway so pointed him out to the peasant and stayed there to hear what would happen. The poor man rushed to him, fell at his feet, and told him his tale of woe. When Father Seraphim had calmed him down he said: "Just keep quiet, and go quickly to the next village, take the road to the right, go behind the fence, and you will find your horse tethered to a post. Take it and go away without saying anything." The peasant rushed off in the direction shown him and did indeed retrieve the animal.'

One day the Staretz spotted a woman among the pilgrims: he called her by name, although he did not know her, and told her to go home straight away: her son was there, waiting for her. When she got back she did, in fact, find her child who had been listed as 'missing' after a battle.

In 1822 a certain Mme Moliaev came to Sarov when her husband, a friend of Father Seraphim, had fallen seriously ill. The Staretz was not receiving anyone that day but was spending it wholly in prayer. All the same, the crowd was waiting in the court. The lady with great difficulty made her way to the front. Suddenly the door opened and the Staretz appeared on the threshold; he called her and gave her holy water and blessed bread, telling her that she and her husband were to share it as soon as she returned. When she got home she found her husband paralysed; with difficulty she made him swallow a little holy water. With that, he found strength to utter, in tears: 'O blessed Seraphim, for the last time you have given me your blessing.' He blessed his wife and children and breathed his last.

What more shall we say? Many monks from various monasteries came to consult the Staretz. He did not readily give his blessing to those who aspired to become superiors and govern souls. 'O how hard this vocation is!' he would say. 'A Superior must have the gift of discerning spirits and understanding man's soul.' But he did predict this office to some who, on the contrary, had no desire for it. There is the case of Father Seraphim putting his staff in a monk's hands and saying: 'When you become abbot your guardian angel will guide you along the way of trials that you will have to endure.' Some years later this monk was appointed superior of a monastery where he had much to suffer.

One day Hieromonk Anthony, superior of a neighbouring monastery (and later, of Zagorsk) came into Father Seraphim's cell while the latter was talking to a merchant, urging him to give up his debauchery. The Staretz spoke to him gently and the man, greatly moved, left the room shedding tears of repentance. Father Anthony, unable to hide his amazement, cried out: 'How can you read the human heart without anything being hidden from you?' 'No, no, my joy,' answered the Staretz, 'the human heart is open to God alone and when one approaches it one finds oneself on the brink of an abyss.' The Hieromonk insisted on discovering the secret of that remarkable intuition which enabled Father Seraphim to recognize sins without anyone's needing to reveal them to him. Then Father Seraphim said, after a moment's silence: 'You see, this man came, like all the others, like yourself, for instance, seeing in me a servant of God, which in fact I am, a wretched and unworthy servant, but a servant all the same; to everyone —as to yourself—I give only what God tells me to give. I believe the first word that comes to me to be inspired by the Holy Spirit and when I start speaking I honestly do not know what lies in the heart of the man who is questioning me. I only know that God directs my words for his benefit. But were I to give an answer out of my own judgement without having previously brought it to God, then I would make a mistake.' And Father Seraphim ended: 'As iron committing itself to the smith I give myself over to God completely and make no move without his will. I do not say anything save what God urges me to say. . . .'

So Seraphim had attained real self-negation, to the transparency of his whole being before the divine will; he let himself be governed not by his own reason but by that other wisdom which, so often, is 'folly' in the eyes of men but wisdom in God's sight (1 Cor. 1. 25).

This gift of insight is closely linked to that of prophecy. By no means did he presume to foretell the future and when anyone pressed him for information concerning political events or the end of the world—which some people thought to be imminent—he answered quietly: 'Who do you think poor Seraphim is? How can anyone as wretched as myself know about such things? I haven't had any revelation about them—as for the day and hour of the end of the world, no one knows that and it is hidden even from the angels. Only the heavenly Father knows it.' And yet when Father Seraphim spoke about the future he seemed to see it spread out before him. Sometimes his radiant expression changed to one of great sadness and tears began to roll down his cheeks. He must have known about the perils that were to overtake Russia and the Church during the last years of the reign of Alexander I. Influences that were hostile to the government of the country spread through the land and unfurled, among them the Decembrist uprising in 1825. Incessant mobilizations then brought army chiefs along the roads that led to Sarov and, if these men happened to visit the Staretz' cell, he never failed to remind them of their obligations towards Church and country.

'God's judgement is coming,' he said, 'because we have strayed from the ways of salvation and have drawn God's wrath upon us. Watch and pray lest the hour come upon you when you do not expect it.' 'Our Church', he said again, 'is now being shaken by trials coming both from abroad and from within our country; enemies are surrounding it on all sides and the Russian people are expecting the supreme sacrifice from you, even at the cost of your life. Your Christian conscience lays this upon you because it is what you are commissioned for. Our Church, of whom Christ is the Head, calls you to action.'

More than once he spoke of the time when Antichrist would come and snatch the crosses from churches and destroy monasteries. 'It will be a time of distress such as has never been since the beginning of the world; the angels of God will hardly have time to gather up the souls from the earth.'

There was the visit of a certain general: when he arrived at the Staretz' cell Father Seraphim let him in and shut the door behind them. Those waiting outside soon heard stifled sobs, then they saw the man emerge, hiding his face in his hands, supported by the father who was carrying his visitor's cap and medals which had rolled on the floor when the general had prostrated himself before him. 'I have crossed Europe during our campaigns,' he said to those present, 'and nowhere have I come across so holy a man.'

The commander of a regiment which, in 1825, had its headquarters in the district of Tambov describes in his diary[3] the amazing reception which he and his wife experienced when they visited Father Seraphim during Easter Week. The general had made the journey simply out of curiosity, persuaded by his ailing wife, but he was overwhelmed by the sight of this old man in a white habit as soon as the latter appeared on his doorstep: 'He seemed like an angel from heaven.' The Staretz came up to him with ineffable gentleness and said: 'You are unhappy, but just pray to the Lord and he will comfort you.' In very fact his superiors' incomprehension vanished and his wife was cured.

Healer, comforter, searcher of the secrets of the heart,

partner in each man's troubles and worries, worker of cures, seer of the future, adviser, teacher—all these charismata came from one and the same source, the presence of the Spirit of Pentecost who continues his action in the world through men of God.

The legend about Father Seraphim's interview with Tsar Alexander I and, shortly afterwards, with his brother the Grand Duke Michael is placed about 1825. The monastery records mention this visit, but nothing about the actual conversation is disclosed. One thing is certain, that the imperial family's devotion to the Staretz endured long after his death. It is good to recall the words of the wife of Tsar Nicholas I on her death-bed: 'I am sure', she said, 'that this little old man will help me to die well.' Seraphim's cloak was sent to her from Sarov and, wrapped in its folds, she passed away peacefully, without suffering.

Father Seraphim was truly the guardian angel of his people; he believed himself responsible for all the evil that lay spread out before him, and that is why his supplications and tears increased in intensity as the number of his sons and daughters grew.

## NOTES

[1] The tradition of startzi, without being an official institution, is a characteristic phenomenon of the Orthodox Church. Tolstoi wrote: 'If the Russian people have still preserved the true image of the living Christ, it is only among the startzi that they have done so.' According to another writer (G. Fedotov): 'He is as close to the hut of the peasant as he is to the palace of the nobleman, to transform the life of each of them.'

[2] The monk George, guestmaster of the monastery, who witnessed this event, recorded the story of this first cure worked by the Staretz.

[3] Published in the *Russian Messenger*, 1879, pp. 267–270.

# 4

# Father of Nuns

THE COMMUNITY OF DIVEYEVO

Father Seraphim, as we have seen, had been brought into a formal relationship with the women's community of Diveyevo which was fairly near the monastery of Sarov. While waiting to become its spiritual father he had never ceased to encourage and foster the vocations of those who sought his advice.

But the position of the community was now becoming increasingly difficult. After Mother Alexandra's death the new Superior—Mother Xenia, a very unyielding woman —proved to be too severe for the nuns. By about 1825 they numbered over fifty and, as the house was very poor, it became almost impossible to feed and clothe them adequately. The money which Mother Alexandra had given to Father Pakhomius remained with the monastery which was responsible for feeding the sisters; but the allowance grew more and more meagre after Father Niphont became superior. Besides, the monks' council had taken a rather harsh line, finding it burdensome for a monastery of men to have an abiding obligation towards Diveyevo. And yet Sarov was tremendously indebted to Mother Alexandra who had financed the building of the cathedral and had given large sums for the upkeep of the monastery. Diveyevo still followed the customs laid down by Father Pakhomius but, in view of the very heavy work which these women had to undertake, the rule had become too burdensome. Ever since Father Seraphim had opened his door nuns kept coming to him and asking him to obtain some alleviation from Mother Xenia. But this Mother Superior (whom he called 'the spiritual scourge') would not listen to him when he asked her to make any changes. 'Look, Father,' she would say to him, 'how can you ask me to change something that Father Pakhomius laid down?' Seeing himself powerless, the father let things pass for the time being, until the moment came when he was forced to intervene in connection with the agreement made with Manturov and the building of a mill. In the meanwhile he sent Mother Xenia the vocations which he discerned, but he also encouraged the founding of other communities, among them that of Ardatov.

This is how a Diveyevo nun describes her first meeting with Father Seraphim: 'The first time I came to Sarov I was only five years old. My mother had an ardent longing to see Father Seraphim. Not many people were there that day and Father opened his door as soon as we said the prayer. He was clothed in white and seemed irradiated with light. "Come in, come in," he said to us. He gave us the icon of the holy Virgin to kiss, and the cross which he wore on his breast, he offered us blessed bread, and gave us his blessing. I was seven when I saw him for the second time. He lifted me up in his arms so that I could kiss the icon. When I was twelve we came to see him again; he asked how old I was and said to my mother: "It's time she was betrothed." My mother smiled and said that I was much too young, but the Staretz insisted. He told my mother to have a white dress made for me and to buy me a pair of red shoes, to wear on feasts of the Lord and of his holy Mother. Each time we returned he spoke to me about my future husband who, as I learned later, was our Lord Jesus Christ. When I was sixteen he told my parents openly that I was to go to Diveyevo, and he went on telling them this until they consented. "The holy Virgin chose her when she was a tiny child," he said. That is how I came to be received into the community of Diveyevo.'

Father Seraphim had a very high opinion of the state of virginity, and he regarded the Virgin Mary as its model. 'To preserve virginity', he would say, 'is not just to refuse marriage but to keep the soul pure and to consecrate oneself to Christ, the heavenly Bridegroom. A virgin who preserves chastity for the love of Christ', he said, 'is like the angels; in becoming espoused to Christ, she is favoured by the Holy Spirit who shows her the way of eternal life.' That is what he ceaselessly taught the nuns. And it is remarkable that in spite of all the difficulties which beset them at this time, there was a very authentic monastic sanctity among many of the young nuns of Diveyevo.[1]

## HELEN MANTUROV

Among others there was Helen Manturov. She was Michael Manturov's younger sister, and after their parents' death he became her tutor. In 1822 she went to Sarov to consult the Staretz about her future. Seventeen years old, with an ardent, passionate temperament which showed itself in her dark eyes, brilliantly gifted and loving balls and gay parties, she had been shattered by her grandfather's death. So much so that she broke off her engagement, retired from the world, and transformed her room into a monastic cell. There she now spent many hours in prayer. According to Father Vassili's account, when Helen told Father Seraphim about her longing to take the veil, the Staretz exclaimed: 'What are you telling me? You, go to a monastery? No, no, my joy, you're going to get married.' Helen burst into tears and went away very unhappy. This did not prevent her from returning to Sarov several times and, each time, she heard the Staretz repeat the same things. 'You are in too much of a hurry, my joy, have a little patience!' Thus did Father Seraphim test her, to strengthen her will and to temper the flights of her impulsive nature. At last he sent for her one day and said: 'Well, my joy, since you are so insistent, go and find Mother Xenia; it's about twelve kilometres from here. You may give it a try.' With a glad heart the girl set out for Diveyevo. There was no room available for her but she was given a little nook which she accepted happily. A month later the Staretz sent for her again. 'The time has come for your engagement', he told her. Helen burst into tears. 'No, no,' he reassured her, 'you've misunderstood me. I was meaning to tell you that the time has come for you to be clothed in the monastic habit. Will you go and tell the superior that Seraphim has decided this? *That's* the Bridegroom I'm talking about.' Beside herself with joy, Helen listened to Father Seraphim's instructions concerning the rule she was to follow and the manual work she was to do. 'In the evening, when you go out to get some fresh air, keep silent and pray in such a way that no one will notice. Begin zealously and persevere patiently until the Bridegroom comes. Watch day and night, and give yourself to continuous prayer for three years; then you will be able to make your vows and you will see your Husband coming.

'When you make your monastic profession you will feel such grace in your heart, such joy! Then, before the icon of the Mother of God, you will say: "Behold the handmaid of the Lord!" Your way is clear in my sight: it will be wholly in God. One thing I warn you: don't want to be a lion, for it's very difficult. I have to be one. But as for you, be a dove! All of you,' he added, thinking of the other sisters of Diveyevo, 'you must all be doves! Now go in peace, and live as I have told you.'

Helen's novitiate lasted for three years: she lived a life of silence, work, and prayer. Sometimes she was to be seen in the evening sitting by her door facing the church, deep in prayer. She learned to spin and weave; unobtrusively she gave her sisters everything that her friends sent her, depriving herself even of necessities. She was appointed reader for the monastery. Sometimes during her night vigils that fear of death which she had experienced so powerfully after her grandfather's death took possession of her. Father Seraphim heard about it and after that he forbade her to keep vigil alone in the church. In 1825, when she was twenty, she made her monastic vows.

## MARY MELIUKOV

What shall we say about little Sister Mary? She came to Sarov for the first time on 21 November 1823. She was thirteen years old and came with her sister Parascovia, whom she absolutely insisted on accompanying to Sarov. The Staretz welcomed her joyfully, and that is how the little girl became a novice at Diveyevo. The sisters spoke of her as 'the child of God' or else 'the angel from heaven who came down from an icon'. She was a silent adolescent with clear blue eyes which she always kept lowered. She was meek and humble and amazed the sisters by the austerity of her life; even Mother Xenia herself, in spite of her austerity, found no fault in her. Father Seraphim himself instructed her in the religious life, and each time that Mary returned from Sarov she seemed transported with joy and, as it were, inwardly illumined. The sisters used to question her, but she never told anyone what passed between the Staretz and herself, in obedience to the orders which he had given her. 'There is nothing greater than obedience,' she was always telling the sisters; and Mary gave a perfect example of it.

One day when she came back from Sarov her elder sister asked her whether she had come across a certain monk. 'What do the monks look like?' asked Mary ingenuously. 'Are they like Father Seraphim?' Her sister answered in amazement, 'What! You so often go to Sarov, and have you really never seen the monks?' 'No,' replied Mary, 'I don't see anything when I go to Sarov because Father Seraphim told me never to raise my eyes. So I wear my cap in such a way that I see only the ground under my feet.'

Like Helen, Mary consecrated her whole life to obedience. She was to die at the tender age of nineteen, after six years of monastic life, bearing with her to the grave most of Father Seraphim's revelations.

40

## XENIA PUTKOV

We must also mention young Xenia Putkov who lived until just before the Saint's canonization and was able to give valuable information about the community of Diveyevo.

Xenia was the daughter of well-to-do parents and they had found a fiancé for her of whom she approved. However, before getting married Xenia wanted to consult the Staretz. His only answer was to send her to make a retreat at Diveyevo. The community's hard life was little to her taste and she fought against the Staretz' orders with all her might. One day when she had disobeyed him she was smitten with remorse and came in tears to make her confession. 'May God forgive you,' he said to her, 'you still belong to me, because I have been praying for you all night, to snatch you from the jaws of the enemy.' It was through this episode that Xenia gave herself wholeheartedly to the religious life. She still had moments of revolt when she would tell the Staretz that she was going to leave him; but he, with almost maternal tenderness, would gently pacify her: 'But where will you go, you little silly? I have begotten you and you can't go away any more.' Xenia was to become one of Seraphim's favourite spiritual daughters, and he gave her important responsibilities. When she accused herself to the father of having a bad-tempered character, the Staretz answered with a touch of gentle irony: 'What are you telling me, my joy? You, a bad character? Indeed, you have the best character in the world, the most perfect character, so gentle, so peaceful!' And he said this in a tone so full of humour that his words had a far greater effect on her than if he had rebuked her.

'Have you been saying your prayers well?' he asked her one day. 'I'm afraid not,' answered Xenia, 'I've always got so much to do that I haven't time to recite them properly.' 'That doesn't matter, my joy,' said the Staretz, 'if you haven't time you can pray while you are working, or as you go from place to place and even in bed, provided you

41

don't forget to call on the Lord in your heart and to prostrate yourself before him morning and evening. If you do this, God himself will help you to attain to perfect prayer.'

## THE MILL

Meanwhile the condition of Father Seraphim's legs was deteriorating, so he obtained permission to go and spend his days in the peace and fresh air of the forest once more. On 25 November 1825 he trod the path to his hermitage which he had not seen since the day, fifteen years ago, when he had been ordered to return to the monastery. Halfway there, at the actual spot where there had once been a spring, now dried up and called the Theologian's Spring (because of the icon of St John the Evangelist which was found there, set on a little pillar) Seraphim stopped to pray. Then, as he was to reveal later, as before he had a vision of the Mother of God, attended by the Holy Apostles Peter and John.[2] The most holy Virgin commanded him to fulfil without delay the promise he had previously made to Mother Alexandra, and to organize a new community; she (the holy Virgin) would be the abbess, and she had shown him seven sisters for it, whom he had sent to Mother Xenia at Diveyevo. The widows, she said, were to continue living at the old community, but there were to be only young girls at the new one. For their upkeep the Staretz was to undertake the building of a mill on the meadow which he had indicated to Manturov, and which he had designated by the stakes.

Then the Virgin Mary touched the dried-up source with her sceptre, causing a flow of limpid water to spring forth. 'This water', she added, 'will work miracles.'

For the next few days Father Seraphim worked at the spring, clearing away the dead leaves which had piled up and surrounding it with a framework, to make a well. Then one morning, 9 December, as he was getting ready to leave his cell and go to the forest, he saw little Mary

Meliukov coming along with another nun named Parascovia (like Mary's sister). Father Seraphim invited them to
come with him to the spring. As they went along Parascovia never ceased coughing; when they came to the spring
the Staretz gave her some water to drink and her coughing
fits stopped immediately. The Virgin's promise began to be
fulfilled. The three of them went on their way to the hermitage; when they reached it the Staretz gave the sisters
some candles which he had brought with him, lit them,
and asked the nuns to pray with him before the cross
fastened to the hut's wall. That prayer together inaugurated the new community of which Parascovia would later
be superior and Mary the spiritual mainstay.

From that day forward and throughout the following
year the father set about preparing all the materials needed
for the building of the mill. With money brought him by
pilgrims he bought timber for the framework and himself
felled trees and sawed them up, planing the beams and
joists. Parascovia and young Mary were made responsible
for negotiating with the owner of the field where the mill
was going to be built, and this man not only made a gift
of it to the community but also added five more acres
of land.

On 9 December 1826 the foundations of the mill were
laid and Sister Xenia was sent to buy the millstones, one
in the neighbouring town of Arzamas, and the other,
secondhand, in a distant village beyond the forest. Sister
Xenia got lost and, as she recounted later, it was the birds
who, circling round and flitting from branch to branch, led
her back to the beaten track.

In the summer of 1827 the mill began to work. The
Staretz sent the seven sisters to live there whom the
Mother of God had chosen. One of them relates: 'When the
mill was built it became our home and we slept there until
the autumn on the two great millstones. They also served
us for the choir and it was on them, too, that we learned
to sing and recite the Psalter. We had to go back to the

refectory of our former community for meals, which was a grief to us. That was why, in the following year, Father Seraphim told us to bake our own bread, which we would bring him to taste.'

'One day when it was my turn to work the mill', another nun relates, 'a strong wind sprang up and the mill's sails were turning powerfully. A tempest was rising. I was afraid and began weeping and inwardly begging Father Seraphim to come and help me. The wind was blowing more and more violently and I couldn't throw my corn in quickly enough. I panicked and threw myself under the millstones to be crushed by them; but they stopped immediately and at the same instant Father Seraphim appeared before me. "You called me, my child," he said, "And I've come to help you." And he quietened me, saying that in future I would even be able to sleep on those millstones without their harming me at all.'

In the month of the following October the Staretz had a dormitory built close to the mill, and then several other buildings. The whole place was called the 'Community of the Mill'. Father Vassili Sadovski was to be its confessor. Father Seraphim loved him very much and esteemed him highly for his goodness and purity of heart.

Sister Parascovia, with whom the Staretz had prayed in the hermitage, was to be 'head miller'. Helen Manturov was the sister whom the Staretz wanted as superior of the community but the young nun, through her great humility, flatly refused this appointment. In spite of her refusal the Staretz urged the sisters not to undertake anything without consulting her, because she was the only educated person among them. The young novices, nearly all of them peasants, were to be seen surrounding her with love and respect, calling her 'our mistress'. Helen instructed the sisters, taught them to read and directed them in the religious life. She would never leave the cell which she had in Mother Xenia's community and she remained there to the last day of her life.

Besides Helen, the young sisters could always find help and comfort from the Staretz. He often used to cite examples of holy monks and nuns for them, and he himself became their model of perfection. 'I have begotten you spiritually,' he would tell them, 'and I shall never forsake you.' 'Those chosen by the Lord during my lifetime are my sisters; those who will come when I am dead will be my daughters.' Everything brought to Father Seraphim by the pilgrims he lavished on them. 'I have sent them vegetable seeds to nourish them and flower plants to gladden them,' he told a friend. 'We have bees too, because it is a good place for them, with water and flowers. And the wax will be useful for making candles.'

## THE NEW WINE

'Have you been to Diveyevo? Have you seen my orphans?' he asked a visitor. 'My virgins are like a swarm of bees; they surround the Queen of Heaven to glorify and serve her.' In receiving only young girls into the new community he thought that they would have less difficulty in being directed than would widows taking the veil. 'I am pouring new wine into new wineskins,' he said, smiling. 'Virgins are as flexible as the branches of birch trees meekly bending in the breeze,' and, straightening up a branch on a young tree, he added: 'This is how they lift up their heads.'

The life of prayer which Father Seraphim had drawn up for his children was of the simplest. In the morning the Our Father three times, the Angelic Salutation three times, the Creed, the morning prayers and twelve invocations with litanies to Christ and the Holy Virgin. During work and while coming and going he advocated the Jesus Prayer. In the evening, after twelve selected psalms, the evening prayers[3] and petitions for the living and the dead. Communion was to be as frequent as possible, and fasting moderate because the Staretz knew that the sisters had to work very hard. So he allowed them to eat as much as they needed and even advised them to put a piece of bread in their pocket when they went to work to prevent dejection when they were weary. 'Even at night', he said, 'put a bit of bread under your pillow; it will make you sleep better.' To protect them from the bitter cold when they were working in the forest the Staretz had a hut built for them with a stove, so that they could come in and get warm. Truly, he watched over every detail, and it can be said that during his lifetime the sisters lacked nothing.

## THE COMMUNITY'S CHURCH

One day towards the end of 1827, when the work of erecting the buildings surrounding the mill was finished, Father Seraphim said to Michael Manturov who frequently came to see him: 'My joy, our poor community hasn't a church yet, and the Holy Virgin wants one built and consecrated to the memory of the nativity of her Son, our Lord Jesus Christ. It must be built on the square in front of Mother Xenia's church; it is fitting that this square should become an altar: Mother Alexandra prayed there long and often and bathed it with her tears.' Manturov immediately started making preparations. Faithful to the Staretz' orders, he had not touched the money accruing from the sale of his estates and the time had now come to use it for God. In fact, the Staretz had several times been offered the money needed for building this church but, each time, he had refused it, saying: 'Some money is the price of wrong, of blood and tears; we must not accept it.' He wished it to be understood that the Lord desired, for his glory, the offering of someone who had divested himself of everything for his Name's sake.[4]

Father Seraphim wished the church to be begun on the feast of our Lord's transfiguration. Everyone was set to work, Michael Manturov had bought the bricks and the sisters brought them to the site which the father had indicated. Mary was one of the first to begin work; while the other sisters took only two or three bricks at a time, she carried five or six of them. 'With silent prayer on her lips it was her ardent soul that was rising skywards,' Father Seraphim said later.

The work took nearly two years and on 6 August 1829 the church was consecrated by Archimandrite Joachim of Nijni-Novgorod. All the texts on this feast of the transfiguration were suggestive of that inner transfiguration which the Staretz so ardently desired for his children.

## MARY'S DEATH

A great sorrow awaited Father Seraphim a few days later. His cell-neighbour, the monk Paul, heard the Staretz weeping; he went to see what was wrong. 'O Paul, if only you knew how great is my grief! Mary has just died!' At the same moment Mary's elder sister, Parascovia, arrived, weeping too, and the father, mastering his grief, tried to comfort her: 'Don't cry, for Mary is in paradise close to the Holy Trinity.' And he added, 'Sister Mary has become Mother Martha, for she has now received the great habit.[5] I have just sent a cloak and everything needed for her burial, so go and make the preparations.' A little later, sisters who had been working in the forest and were passing through Sarov came in; they were stunned and dismayed to hear the sad news, for they had seen Mary that same day before they set out for work. Mary had worn herself out on the building of the church. The Staretz sent a coffin hollowed out of a solid oak, and money to be distributed to the poor in her memory. They left on her head the little green velvet cap embroidered with gold thread which the Staretz had given her when she entered the monastery and which she wore on Sundays. Her body was wrapped in the black cloak and scapular, a black veil covered her face, and in her hands was the rosary which Father Seraphim had given her. Her body was laid beside Mother Alexandra's tomb.

Not long after the funeral Mary's elder brother, Ivan Meliukov, who was the monastery's watchman, came to find Father Seraphim to tell him of his decision to become a monk. Their conversation lasted three hours. Ivan related afterwards that when the Staretz spoke about Mary his face was lit by so dazzling a light that he could not look at him without shielding his eyes. 'If only you knew, my joy,' said the father, 'the ineffable grace which Mary obtains from the Lord! Your whole family will be inundated with it . . . Mother Martha is a true saint and her prayers will bring great blessings on your descendants and on the community.'[6]

## THE CRYPT

After the church was built the foundations were dug for a crypt in honour of the Mother of God. Four pillars were to support the vault, and Father Seraphim saw these as prefiguring the four bodies which would rest there in time to come.

On 8 September 1830 the work was finished and the dedication celebrated.

The care of the two churches was entrusted to Helen and Xenia. 'Everything to do with the church', the Staretz told them, 'is like an inner fire enkindling us, and looking after it is the best work of all. The humblest job, be it only to clean the floor of the house of God, is a nobler work than all the others. Everything you do in the house of God should be done with love and reverence. You must do nothing trivial there, only necessary duties. For where else could you find greater joy than in the place where our Lord is dwelling, surrounded by cherubim and seraphim and all the heavenly spirits!'

At all hours, even during the night, the sisters were to keep a rota for reciting the psalms and so pray without ceasing for the living and the dead. And 'the angel of the Lord will watch over the community'.

The chronicles of Diveyevo also give us some very poignant details: one day while Xenia was cleaning the church she noticed that the lamp which was always kept burning before the icon had gone out, and there was no more oil for relighting it, neither was there any money with which to buy some. She began weeping: 'If we are without oil even now, what's going to happen later?' And she started doubting Father Seraphim's words concerning his promise of prosperity. Then, as she left the church, she saw a peasant coming up to her: 'Are you the sacristan?' he asked her. He gave her 300 rubles for the lamp in memory of his parents. She recounted later: 'During Father Seraphim's lifetime the pilgrims always brought us enough money for the upkeep of the church; they even sent magnificent bells from Nijni-Novgorod and patens and chalices from Moscow.'

## THE DOWER OF THE QUEEN OF HEAVEN

Timber was also bought for the building of the refectory. 'It will be the residence of a great Lady;' said the Father, 'everything must be ready beforehand and when she comes to live with you, you will wait on her.' The sisters asked themselves who this 'Lady' might be. It was only after Father Seraphim's death when the icon of the Virgin of Tenderness—before which he had passed to God—was brought to the refectory, that the sisters remembered his words. The Staretz named this icon 'Joy of all joys' and he loved to call himself her 'servant'. He used to sing the Easter hymns before her: 'Rise, shine, O new Jerusalem, for the glory of the Lord has risen upon you. . . .'

This new Jerusalem was in his eyes the little Community of the Mill whose abbess was the Mother of God.

'If you knew what a haunt of Satan this district used to be,' said the father, 'but God has been pleased to hear our prayer and drive the demon from these parts.' 'I declare and take the Lord for my witness that there is not a single stone in this community which has been laid through my own will; not one order has been given out of my own head, not a single sister has been received save by order of our most holy Lady, the Mother of God. She it is who directs, instructs and protects her garden.'[7]

The Staretz wanted to surround this dower of the Virgin

with a moat three metres wide and three metres deep. The sisters would have preferred an enclosure wall, but the father replied, 'How silly you are! This moat will recall and mark out the path which the feet of the Queen of Heaven trod when she walked round the land to take possession of it!' In the meanwhile the sisters were not at all disposed to set to work on it until the day when one of them, working late into the night, suddenly saw Father Seraphim, clad in his white habit; by the light of a candle he was breaking the earth with a pick-axe. In dismay she dashed to the dormitory to wake the sisters, who came running out and did indeed see the light but found no one there. Nevertheless the clods of earth and the tool bore witness to the apparition. That same night another sister who had been working in the forest was sleeping in the little hut which the father had built for them. She got up very early and saw the Staretz beckoning to her: 'Go quickly and tell the sisters to go on digging the moat which I've begun.' All the way back to Diveyevo the sister was asking herself: 'How could the Father have been at Diveyevo when he's now in the forest?' But she had hardly arrived there before her companions told her about the Staretz' mysterious appearance and of how he suddenly vanished. They could not account for it, yet they understood that Father Seraphim himself wanted to begin that work which seemed so important to him.

So they set to work. Helen, pick in hand, directed the operations. The father had built her a shelter from the sun because she suffered from violent headaches. Even in winter the sisters did not stop working; Father Seraphim ceaselessly urged them on because he was afraid he might die before the work was finished. He did, in fact, die soon after its completion.

## PLAN FOR A CATHEDRAL

One day, kneeling on the floor in his cell by the block of wood which he used as a table, Father Seraphim sketched

the plan of a cathedral before the wondering eyes of Manturov and Father Vassili. He had already spoken to young
Mary about this cathedral but now its details were beginning to take shape. 'On Mother Alexandra's land, outside
the moat, a monastery will be organized', he said, 'where
widows will be received; but our community will be inside
the moat and will receive young girls. In between them
a cathedral will rise up, consecrated to the Holy Trinity.
It will be our Jerusalem. A high white wall will surround
it and five domes will crown it, to symbolize Christ and the
four Evangelists.' Then he combined some enigmatic
words with the technical details he was giving: he spoke of
relics, of Easter chants being sung at midsummer, of visits
from the imperial family to these places,[8] of a great bell
from Moscow which, when it rang out for the first time
(and Father Seraphim in his deep voice imitated the sound
of the bell), would waken the whole world and himself as
well. 'O, what joy, what joy there will be then,' he said,
'and that crowd, that crowd of believers!' 'But', he added,
'that joy will be of short duration.' And his expression
clouded, although it was usually so limpid; he bent his head
and tears began to roll down his cheeks.

To what was he referring when he said these things?
It was thought that the allusions to 'Easter hymns' and the
'crowd of believers' were connected with Father Seraphim's
canonization which was to take place in the summer of
1903. Others saw in them a prophecy of the last days and
the end of the world. 'You will not live to see Antichrist,'
he told the sisters, 'but you will see the beginning of his
reign. . . . What distress, what distress there will be!'
Nevertheless the triumphant note of the resurrection pre-
dominated in his words when he stated that the whole
world and himself as well 'would awaken' at the sound of
the bell from Moscow.

This cathedral which he desired to consecrate to the
Holy Trinity would be the crowning work of his endeavour;
it was to be, as it were, the revelation of the plenitude of

51

the Creator's work. Father Seraphim seemed to be following the example of St Sergius of Radonezh who, in the fourteenth century, had built a little church near Moscow in honour of the Trinity—to strengthen his brethren, he declared, in union of love after the image of the Triune God.

The community of the Mill was to symbolize the glorious transfiguration of the world through love.

## NOTES

[1] The main sources for the piecing together of their biographies are the memoirs of Father Vassili Sadovski (b. 1800), parish priest of Diveyevo and later spiritual father of the community.

[2] How are we to explain the presence—always the same—of these apostles with the Mother of God? St Seraphim gave no explanation of it and there would, perhaps, be no point in trying to find one, were we not aware of the importance the saint gave to the event of the Lord's resurrection and did we not remember that these two disciples were the first to bear witness to it. The first two occasions when Seraphim saw them with the Mother of God were at the moment when, after long illness, he was reborn to new life. And now he was going to be told of the rebirth of a community of virgin nuns.

[3] Orthodox morning and evening prayers form a short office quite distinct from the long offices chanted in monasteries. The 'litanies' are short phrases, not the long western form of litany.

[4] The whole story of this building is faithfully recorded by Father Vassili Sadovski.

[5] The 'great habit' is conferred on monks and nuns practising continuous silence and a very strict rule. A new name is given them to signify their advance into the life of God.

[6] Ivan had three daughters and one of them, Helen, then six years old, had been entrusted to the care of her aunts Parascovia and Mary. The Staretz loved her and predestined her as a bride for Nicholas Motovilov.

[7] We should note that the Orthodox people regard the abbeys of Kiev and Athos—as well as the city of Jerusalem—as the dower of the Mother of God. Father Seraphim added the community of Diveyevo to them, predicting that it would one day become an abbey where a thousand sisters would find their sphere of service to the Lord and his Mother.

[8] During the canonization of Father Seraphim in 1903 the imperial family was, in fact, present at the ceremonies at Sarov and Diveyevo.

# 5

# The Pilgrim Throngs at Sarov

## FATHER SERAPHIM'S VISITORS

Devotion to Father Seraphim was increasing more and more. He drew people from all classes and conditions, sometimes as many as two thousand in one day. They usually came by the Arzamas road and there was incessant coming and going of vehicles of all kinds: luxurious carriages with costly teams of horses, ordinary coaches, peasants' carts. Many people arrived on foot as well, staff in hand, bundle on their back. Sometimes they covered hundreds of kilometres and walked for weeks, often having taken the vow of a wandering pilgrim, going from one holy place to another in search of a Jerusalem when they could not go to the Holy Land.[1] The great crowds coming to Sarov stayed in the monastery guest houses, in neighbouring taverns, in peasant huts, and often during the summer they spent the nights under the stars. Sometimes they waited several days before being able to see the Staretz. At dawn, as soon as the bells of Sarov rang out, the pilgrims surged into the monastery court like ocean waves. With that amazing variety of dialects, types, dress and colour, everyone was trying to get nearer to the steps leading to Father Seraphim's cell. They knew that the sacraments were brought to him on festivals and that after receiving Communion he spent long hours in prayer, as he did also on Wednesdays and Fridays when he kept his door shut the whole day. But when he appeared in his doorway everyone craned to see him better. 'Come along, come along, my joys!' he would say. 'Christ is risen.' That was his usual greeting. But he would also pick out someone or other lost

53

in the crowd: 'Your turn now, my daughter,' he called to a poor woman afraid to come forward. 'I've something to say to you,' he told another, calling her by her name. And the procession began. 'And you, where do you think you're going?' he called out to a young peasant who was elbowing his way through the throng while held back by an invisible power. Suffocating and perspiring he threw himself at the Staretz' feet and, without taking any notice of the crowd, began confessing his sins.

We read a story in a periodical about the visit of a young man, who was really still a child: the Staretz' way of putting pieces of bread dipped in wine into his visitors' mouths by means of a long wooden spoon struck him as so comical that he could not stop laughing. His mother sent him out with a scolding, and then later told him to go back to the Staretz and apologize. The child found the Father alone and reading, sitting on a coffin which he had had brought into his cell. 'O it's you, my friend,' he said kindly, 'do you read the Gospels?' When the boy replied that in his family it was thought that only the clergy had authority for such reading, the Staretz opened his Gospels and read the text of Matt. 7. 1–2: 'Judge not, that you be not judged.' This saying affected the boy profoundly and he often came back to Sarov to see Father Seraphim. When he could not come near the Staretz because of the crowds, it was enough to see him from afar; his conscience would awake and a longing to pray welled up within him.

When people asked the Staretz' advice about duty to their neighbour he used to say: 'Do what the Lord has taught us; he will require a reckoning for it on the last day: "I was hungry and you gave me food, I was thirsty and you gave me drink, I was a stranger and you welcomed me, I was naked and you clothed me, I was sick and you visited me, I was in prison and you came to me." '

With people coming to make their confession it was love towards God and neighbour that the Staretz chiefly sought in the human heart, without taking too much notice of those virtues and vices which penitents sometimes displayed. He was concerned with the whole man, his joys and sufferings, much more than with the unintentional sins which might have been committed. His compassion when faced with grief and suffering was characteristic of his spirit. Likewise his counsel was simple and full of kindness: 'Be upright,' he would say, 'maintain peace in your soul and be loving towards others.' Or again, 'Give the spirit what is due to it and the body what it needs, so that the body can carry the spirit along the way of salvation.' Or again, 'In the spiritual life do nothing beyond your strength but always take the middle way, for this is the royal road.'

The monastery's great court was filled with sick folk, paralytics were carried, the blind and the possessed were led and every day Seraphim healed them.

There was a paralytic child, his small emaciated body nothing but skin and bones. His parents had made a long journey on foot, hoping for a miracle. They waited their turn there in the court for hours; the father was intent on other sick folk. But there he was, leaving his cell, making his way through the crowd and drawing near; he took the child up in his arms and kissed him, then gave him back to his mother, telling her to pray without ceasing for the cure of her little one. And the Staretz moved on to other sick folk. It was later learned that the little child was restored to health. He did not like spectacular cures; he looked for faith and asked for prayer.

Then again there was a little blind child; for five long days the parents had been waiting for the Staretz to come out, for he had been in retreat without receiving anyone. When at last they were able to reach the father he breathed on the boy's eyes and the child felt as though a veil had fallen from them. Not long after, he completely recovered his sight.

The deaf man whose ears Father Seraphim anointed with oil prostrated himself before him to thank him, but the Staretz protested: 'It is not I, but the Lord's Mother who has cured you.'

It would be tedious to enumerate all his miraculous cures. Yet one of them seems quite exceptional: it happened to the wife of a man called Vorotilov, a friend of Father Seraphim. In the middle of the night Vorotilov ran to the Staretz to tell him that his wife was in her death agony. In spite of the late hour the Staretz was sitting by his door as though expecting him. Vorotilov besought him with tears to heal his wife, but the father replied that he could do nothing, the time had come for her to leave the world. The man, on his knees, went on beseeching him. Then the Staretz plunged into profound prayer and a little later told his friend, 'All right, my joy, go home in peace, the Lord has granted you this grace: your wife will live.' When he got home Vorotilov did indeed find that his wife had been cured at the very hour when the Staretz had prayed to the Lord.

Sometimes Father Seraphim shut himself in his cell for whole days at a time to obtain God's forgiveness for some soul in spiritual distress. He attached great importance to intercession: it took precedence over everything. 'Forgive me, my joy,' he said to someone whom he received only at the end of the day, 'I've kept you waiting, but I had to pray for a lost soul.'

One day a sister came to him while he was praying; she found his cell plunged in pitch darkness although the sun was shining. There was not even any light from the candles. 'Perhaps they've gone out,' she thought. A chill air penetrated the darkness and her heart as well. The sister, remembering that the Staretz used to say, 'The devil is cold,' fell to the ground, terrified. 'It's Satan paying me back,' she then heard, 'he wanted to destroy a soul I was praying for, but God would not let him. So Satan is in a rage and that's why he's made it so dark.'

Father Seraphim often identified himself with those who came to him. He once said to someone who was tortured by the thought that God might not forgive his transgressions: 'Now don't be afraid, the Lord is good; he will forgive all sins, mine and yours, and will grant salvation to us both.'

A woman penitent, who reached Sarov after a long journey, sleepless nights and fatigue, came to the father with a burning desire to make her confession. The first words she heard were those of absolution. Confused and feeling herself unworthy, she fell on her knees weeping; and Father Seraphim, taking her hands in his, knelt beside her and went on with the prayer of absolution. And then that woman felt a blessing within her, such as she had never experienced before.

Another time they were trying to draw the Staretz' attention to a professor who was longing to speak to him, but the father went on attending to others without even glancing at the man, who was an eminent teacher of philosophy. When he did finally speak to him the Staretz said: 'Teaching others is like casting stones down from the belfry, whereas putting into practice what one teaches is like carrying those stones up to the top of the belfry.' It was not that Father Seraphim underestimated mental attainment, far from it. He appreciated education and often told pastors not to lose sight of their duty to teach. But he loved humility and integrity of life.

When some parents came to see him about their children and doubted his intellectual ability, Father Seraphim, discerning their thoughts, said teasingly: 'But who am I, poor me, beside your great intellect?'

Father Seraphim did not use extraordinary means to bring people to God. His words which could sometimes be sharp roused the most hardened spirits, stirred the most dormant conscience.

Among the milling crowds at Sarov we may single out a few faces that we shall see again. There is little Helen who is Ivan Melioukov's daughter and Mary's niece. She was still very young when her aunts Parascovia and Mary brought her to the father; but in her memoirs which are preserved in the *Chronicles of Diveyevo* she recalls and describes how the Staretz took her in his arms, put her on the table, and told the Diveyevo sisters who were with her to bow to her, 'because she is going to be your guardian,' he said. 'She is an angel in soul and body,' he added. Little Helen was still far from realizing that she was destined not for the monastic life but for marriage with a man who was to be the Staretz' devoted servant and the guardian of the community of Diveyevo. This visit and the Staretz' attitude to the child had a prophetic meaning, considering the fact that it happened a few months before Helen's future husband, Nicholas Motovilov, came to Sarov.

## PELAGIA

Another person to attract our attention is blessed Pelagia, a young woman of nineteen who was brought to Sarov in 1828 by her mother and husband to be cured of so-called madness. The Staretz seemed to be waiting for her. He dismissed his visitors: 'Go in peace, go in peace,' he said to them and then took the young woman into his cell and spent several hours with her. When the husband returned, impatiently looking for his wife, he beheld the Staretz respectfully conducting her to the door, giving her a rosary, bowing to the ground before her and saying: 'Go to Diveyevo, Mother, and watch over my orphans.' When she had gone he turned to the people waiting outside and said: 'That woman will be a flaming torch of holiness and will bring many souls to God.'

At the sight of the rosary in his wife's hands the husband exclaimed angrily: 'Isn't this Staretz mad as well? Where is his so-called insight, when he gives a rosary to a married woman and sends her to Diveyevo?'[2]

Pelagia had chosen the way of folly for Christ. She left her husband who used to beat her and chain her up to keep her in the house and, in 1837, she was received by the nuns of Diveyevo. For forty-seven years she lived a life of asceticism and continuous prayer in the monastery, endowed with a gift of insight which was remarkable for the unusual character of its manifestations. She died at Diveyevo, surnamed 'Seraphim's seraph', so clearly did she live in the light of the holy Staretz.

On another day there came an old hermit, the monk Timon, a friend of Seraphim's youth, and they had not seen one another for twenty years. Timon waited all day long in the crowd. When evening fell and Seraphim welcomed him to his cell, the old hermit wept at seeing his friend again. 'O Father,' he cried, 'why wouldn't you let me come to you? Are you holding anything against me?' Father Seraphim lovingly reassured him: 'You've seen all those sick and handicapped people? They must be cared for first, because it is the sick, is it not, who need a physician? Now the time is my own, I am all yours, and we can chat at leisure.' And they spent the night talking.

When it was time for them to part, Father Seraphim said to his friend: 'Sow, Father Timon, sow the corn you are given, sow it everywhere and whenever you can. Sow it in the good soil, sow it in the sand, sow it on the rock, by the wayside and among the thorns. There is always hope that a seed may germinate and grow and bear fruit, even if it is only after some time. Do not bury the talent you are given but put it in the bank to gain interest.'[3]

## NOTES

[1] While encouraging genuine pilgrims, the authorities nevertheless took steps to reduce these movements of working people who undertook long journeys after the harvests each season.

[2] The Orthodox rosary, quite different from the western one, is given with the religious habit and denotes an obligation to the Jesus Prayer.

[3] The idea of talents that were to bear spiritual fruit never left Father Seraphim. He himself had been the good and faithful servant who rendered to his Lord the fruits of those gifts which he had received in such abundance.

# 6

# A Further Call to the Desert

## THE NEAR HERMITAGE

It will soon be noticed that Father Seraphim kept leaving
the monastery to return to the forest where for so many
years he had lived in intimacy with God. He was often to
be seen working by the spring or else by the river Sarovka.
The Staretz was, in fact, surrounding the spring with stones
which he fetched from the river in order to protect the flow
of water. So there he was, carrying his sack of stones and
staggering under the heavy load. 'I'm tormenting him who
torments me,' he said jovially to those who commiserated
with him.[1]

Meanwhile funds were collected and a shelter was built for
him close to the spring, which had now become a fountain
with a pool. This hut was named Father Seraphim's Near
Hermitage.

While it was being built, the Staretz once said to Xenia:
'Look, my joy, this shelter is for you as well, because you
will all be using it one day.' It was only after the Staretz'
death that Xenia understood the meaning of these words,
when the hut was brought to Diveyevo as a relic. It was
built two miles from Sarov; the father spent the whole day
there working and praying, only returning to the monastery
at nightfall. But he spent Sundays and festivals at the
monastery. He divided his time between these two places.
Pilgrims were waiting for him now at Sarov, now at the
spring; yet more lay in wait for him as he set out or on his
way back. So at length, to free himself from the crowds,
the Staretz often rose while it was still night to reach his

hermitage before sunrise; and the wild animals took to coming to him again.[2]

## THE BEAR

One day Matrona, one of the nuns, saw him sitting on a tree trunk in the company of a bear. Terrified, she let out a scream. The Staretz turned round and, seeing her, patted the animal and sent him away. Then he invited Matrona to come and sit beside him. 'But', Matrona relates, 'hardly had we sat down when the animal returned from the wood and came and lay at the Staretz' feet. I was as terrified as before, but when I saw Father Seraphim, quite unconcerned, treating the bear like a lamb, stroking him and giving him some bread, I calmed down. I looked at the father and was dazzled by the sight of his face which seemed to me full of light and like an angel's. When I was wholly reassured the Staretz gave me a piece of bread and said: "You needn't be the least afraid of him, he won't hurt you." So I held out the bread to the bear and, while he was eating it, it was such joy to be feeding him that I wanted to go on doing so. Seeing how much I was enjoying it, Father Seraphim said: "You remember the story of St Jerome feeding a lion in the desert? Well, here we've got a bear obeying us." I exclaimed: "The sisters would die of fright if they saw such a sight!" "They won't see it," replied the Staretz. Then, "I'd be very sad if anyone killed him," I went on. "Nobody will kill him and nobody except yourself will see him," answered the father.' Matrona was already rejoicing at the thought of telling the sisters about it but the Staretz, reading her thoughts, said to her, 'No, my joy, you're not to tell anyone until eleven years after my death. Then God will show you whom to tell.'

And so it happened: a day came when, some years after the father's death, Matrona went past an artist's studio in the monastery; he was working on a portrait of the father in the forest on a tree trunk. 'O,' she said, 'you really must paint the bear!' 'What bear?' asked the artist in surprise.

Then Matrona told him the story and remembered the Staretz' words. Eleven years had gone by.

## CHILDREN

Meanwhile the forest was increasingly becoming a place of pilgrimage. The father consecrated Wednesdays and Fridays wholly to prayer, and in order to be undisturbed he had dug a pit behind his stove where he used to hide. On the other days he was at everybody's disposal.

He had a specially tender love for children and, since his affection for them was well known, they were often sent to knock on his cell door and the father could never resist them.

Here is one testimony, among others, from the sister of the Russian philosopher Constantine Aksakov,[3] who met Father Seraphim when she was small. When her parents arrived at the monastery they were told that the Staretz was in the forest. 'I very much doubt whether you've much chance of seeing him,' said Abbot Niphont, 'at least, not unless he hears the voices of your children. Take them with you and send them on ahead!' There were about twenty children at Sarov that day, who had come with their parents. Everyone took the superior's advice and they set out for the forest.

'It became darker and darker, and more and more dense,' writes N. Aksakov. 'We were afraid. Luckily a ray of sunshine shone through the branches, and with it our courage revived. Then we ran towards a glade bathed in sunlight; we saw there, beside a fir tree, a little hunchbacked old man deftly hacking at the tall undergrowth around the base of a tree. When he heard us coming he cocked his ear and darted into the thicket. Then, breathless, he looked at us and hid again in the undergrowth. We lost sight of him. Then all twenty of us children called to him in chorus: "Father Seraphim, Father Seraphim!" At the sound of our voices he could hide himself no longer and his white head soon appeared above the greenery. Finger on lips, he seemed to be imploring us not to give him away to the grown-ups. He came towards us and sat down on the ground, motioning us to come and join him. Our little Liz was the first to run into his arms, burying her rosy face on his shoulder. "O my treasures, O my treasures," the Staretz kept on saying, tenderly folding us each to his heart in turn. Then, when he had to go and meet the crowd, we stayed and watched, lying in the grass.' On the way back little Liz said to her sister: 'You know, Father Seraphim only looks like an old man, but he's really a child like us.'

Many are the stories of pilgrims coming to see the man of God in his solitude.[4] One of them, a young widow, Anne Eropkine, describes her pilgrimage in 1830. True, she had been to Sarov before, but when she heard that the Staretz was in the forest she sped there 'like a hind', as she writes. She saw Father Seraphim from afar, up to his knees in water in the river; he was drawing stones from it and piling them up on the bank. A dense crowd was gathering. When he saw the young woman Seraphim called out to her: 'O good, you've come back, my treasure!' It looked like being a fine day, yet the father urged the pilgrims to return to Sarov. However, no one wanted to part from him. Then, towards evening, a terrible storm broke, drenching them all. The next day the young woman came back to see the father again; he met her with a smile: 'Well, my joy, what a storm, what a cloudburst! If you had obeyed me yesterday, my treasure, and had gone back as I told you to, you wouldn't have got soaked.' In his cell she noticed a big candle burning before the icon; Father Seraphim told her: 'This candle was brought by a good man during the storm, and I lit it beseeching God to turn from his holy wrath. Indeed, everything at Sarov might have been destroyed, so great was God's anger with the monastery.'

Anne also said, at the end of her story, that she had the great joy of hearing Father Seraphim speak some amazing words about the Kingdom of God and eternal life. 'I could not repeat', she writes, 'either the father's actual words or

the impression they made on me; I shall only say that the
expression on his face seemed so extraordinary: a light shone
from within, illuminating his features, his whole being
seemed enfolded in the grace of the Holy Spirit and raised
above the earth. He spoke to me about the heavenly joys
of those who have a share in God's glory. It was as though
he himself was actually living all this at that very moment,
partaking of this bliss and enabling me to live it with him.
He seemed unable to find words to express what he was
experiencing, so he ended: "O my joy, such bliss, such
beatitude, I cannot describe it all!" '

Another account tells us that Father Seraphim often besought the Lord to grant him the grace of contemplating
'the mansions of the Father's house' (John 14. 2) and that
this was granted to him. Thus he became 'all glance, all
eye', 'like the cherubim and seraphim' (Abba Bessarion).

### TRIALS
However it is only too true that the joy of God is the
daughter of agony. Seraphim was to be led to the cross, he
who followed and imitated the Lamb of God. Trials were
to assail him from all sides. Just when the father seemed to
have attained a very high degree of sanctity, enemy voices
arose against him and his work, coming from the world as
well as from within the monastery.

First and foremost there was the envy of Ivan Tikhonovitch.[5] One day this man asked Father Seraphim to introduce him to the community of Diveyevo in the capacity of
choir master. In the end, after much hesitation, the Staretz
yielded to his request. Then, taking advantage of his title,
Ivan began introducing to Diveyevo the new trends inspired by Italian music which was then all the vogue.
Everything traditional in monastic chant seemed to him old
fashioned. 'O how it grieves me!' said the Father to Manturov. 'Look how he's bringing this new way of singing
here!' The 'painter of Tambov' was also beginning to
initiate the sisters in another way of painting icons.

Noticing Father Seraphim's friendship with Manturov, Ivan tried to ingratiate himself with the latter, inviting him to come and take tea with him, and visiting him. This worried Father Seraphim and he warned Manturov of Ivan's intentions. 'Ivan is cold,' he told him, 'all his life his heart will be cold towards others and he will only cause you trouble.'

Once when the Staretz was sitting with a nun by the spring he drew her attention to the water: clear and limpid a moment ago, it suddenly tossed and boiled. In amazement the sister asked Seraphim why it had changed like that. At that instant along came Ivan, walking down the slope towards them. 'That's the reason,' the father then said, pointing to Ivan, 'he has overthrown poor Seraphim, and he's even going to overthrow your community.'

Ivan Tikhonovitch regarded the Staretz as an unpractical person, remote from earthly realities; that was, moreover, the opinion of many representatives of the clergy (as can be seen from the letter of Bishop Arsen who knew the Staretz and had opportunity to convince himself of his sanctity). Ivan made no attempt to hide his intentions of supplanting the man of God in looking after the community. 'You are getting old,' he said to Father Seraphim, 'leave the community to me!' He had also drawn up plans for the future cathedral, the construction of which would involve demolishing some of the buildings erected by the Staretz and levelling the Virgin's Path, and had begun negotiations with some people of influence to raise the community to the rank of monastery.[6] The sisters numbered about 100, and Mother Xenia's community about 150. Ivan Tikhonovitch felt that they should be reunited into a single community and that they would thus obtain the necessary rights and subsidies. Father Seraphim thought it was too early for this and said to the sisters: 'Yes, you will have the rights and title of a monastery and all that goes with it one day, but don't do anything to obtain it, don't go out and beg, but live by the work of your hands, cultivate your fields and

65

vegetable gardens, and let prayer be your chief occupation.'

Ivan also had pretensions towards the priesthood and when he was refused ordination he betook himself to another monastery where he was led to hope that he might succeed. On his return he went to announce his decision to the Staretz; he found the latter beside the spring, pouring water over his feet and hands and head. 'You will never see Seraphim's face again,' was all that the man of God would say to him. And he dismissed Ivan who, meeting Manturov, described the scene to him. Manturov hastened to the spot; he found the father still pouring water over his hands, feet and head with a piece of birch bark. 'I call you to witness', he told Manturov, 'that I've done all I can to turn Ivan from his schemes, but I have not succeeded; I take no responsibility for his soul. As you see, I wash my feet and my hands and my head of him.'

And this is what happened. The Governor General of Moscow, Count Zakrevsky, and his mother-in-law owned lands in the vicinity of the monastery of the Mill. These were being exploited by a steward who would not tolerate the donation of part of them to the community. Filled with rage, he made a scurrilous report about the sisters; the Governor believed it and came hurling insults at Mother Xenia, who fainted at the attack.

There must have been weightier reasons than merely personal ones for the Governor of Moscow to behave in this way. These reasons, which are not given in the *Chronicles of Diveyevo*, might be formulated as follows: at this period serfdom had not yet been abolished and there were frequent instances of escape. Since it was easy for the latter to find asylum in monasteries they often took refuge there. In Father Seraphim's day there was an actual instance of a girl who escaped from a noble estate in the neighbourhood, clothed herself as a nun and led a vagrant life. When she was arrested she justified herself by saying that she had Father Seraphim's permission to do so. That is why the civil authorities were on their guard and vilified the community of Diveyevo which as yet had no legal status and was not formally recognized by the state.

The incident which took place during the Governor's visit to Diveyevo was reported to Father Seraphim; he told Manturov to write to the Count, not to reprove him but to thank him for his kindness to the sisters. This extraordinary action was, as we shall see, a further proof of the Staretz' astonishing intuition. For at Moscow the Governor ordered an investigation concerning the sisters and the father himself, which was carried out by the civil as well as by the religious authorities. These enquiries resulted in total exoneration, and the community even received the right of legal existence from the authorities. And it was for this that Father Seraphim wanted to thank the Governor.

Meanwhile worse trials were awaiting the father and the community of sisters. The opposition came mainly from ecclesiastical ranks. When the monks once told the father that he was causing scandal by admitting women to his cell, Seraphim did not take it very seriously; he said that he could not do anything else, because if people came to ask for his spiritual help it was his duty to give it them, since he had to answer for this before the Lord's seat of judgement.

He took no notice of recriminations so long as they were directed only at himself, but answered with a smile: 'For myself, I'm not in the least scandalized at scandalizing everyone.' It was only when the accusations fell on the sisters that he broke his silence: 'They are attacking wretched Seraphim,' he told young Xenia one day. 'They are blaming him for permitting young girls to spend the night in the church reciting the psalms. "Such a thing has never been seen before," they say. And my answer is: "If only you could see the angelic hosts surrounding them and assisting them while they pray!" ' That silenced them but not for long, for the slanderers' attacks became fiercer still. 'O what our Staretz endured for us,' Xenia related, 'but he bore it all with patience and goodness.'

One day the superior himself, Abbot Niphont, stopped Seraphim in the monastery court and told him that his relations with the sisters could not go on. Seraphim bowed to the ground and answered him quietly: 'You are a pastor; do not let yourself be influenced by false witnesses, do not listen to what is told you in spite. Life eternal is our aim in all things, so do not block the way to it by pettiness. You are a pastor,' he told him a second time, 'let your words be worthy of what you proclaim!'

After that Niphont directed his attacks at the sisters. Under his influence the monastery's administrative council made application to the civil authorities for a garrison of soldiers to watch the Holy Gate of the monastery, through which the sisters continually passed on their way to Father Seraphim, who supplied them with fuel and food. The civil authorities provided soldiers who were to prevent this. 'Everyone knew that the monks disliked Father Seraphim on our account', relates Mother Eudoxia, 'because he supplied us with food.' But this is how the father outwitted the monks.

'One day when I was with Father Seraphim,' Mother Eudoxia tells us again, 'he gave me a large sack and told me to return to Diveyevo by way of Sarov's Holy Gate. He usually advised me to make a detour in order to avoid the soldiers. I was astonished that, this time, he was mercilessly sending me into harm's way. (The Abbot and monks had, in fact, ordered the soldiers to stop us going through and it was I in particular whom they had told the soldiers to intercept, because I used to come more frequently than the others to fetch our provisions.) Not daring to disobey, I shouldered my burden without so much as knowing what it contained, and off I went. When I got to the Gate I said my prayer; at the same instant the soldiers seized my sack and took me to the Abbot, who ordered me to open it. My hands were trembling; he was watching me without saying a word. When I opened the sack what was my surprise to see it filled with stones, crusts of bread, bits of wood, old

68

sandals, all this crammed so full that it was a ton weight! Taken aback, Niphont exclaimed: "O Seraphim, it's not enough for you to mortify yourself, you have to torment the Diveyevo sisters as well!" And he let me go. Another time the father again gave me a load of stones and sand and said to me: "This will be the last time that they will stop you." And indeed, I was stopped as I went through the Gate and taken to Niphont. When he saw the stones he told the soldiers not to stop me any more. After that I could go through the Holy Gate as often as I liked.'

The Staretz would smile when the sisters told him these stories because, although his heart grieved him, he always looked on the humorous side when with his 'orphans'. But unfortunately it was not only the Holy Gate which was being watched; even the woods of Sarov were patrolled by forest guards who had been told to stop the sisters from picking wild strawberries or gathering mushrooms.

A guard once raised his whip and was about to strike one of the sisters; his whip was snatched from him by a mysterious power and disappeared, and he could not find it again. 'How do you suppose he could find it,' said Father Seraphim chuckling, 'when the whip is buried in the bowels of the earth?' Then the sisters realized that the Staretz' love and prayers were protecting them wherever they went.

But the outrages became increasingly hard to bear: Father Seraphim was accused of theft.

'While the mill was being built', Xenia relates, 'we were brought two pieces of wood that were not worth anything, and these were left at our door. Hardly had these stumps been put there when along came the monks. "Your Seraphim is stealing everything from us," they cried. "Show us where you have hidden the wood!" We showed them the two stumps but they would not believe us and went on molesting us. So then I ran to the father and before I had opened my mouth he said, "Yes, yes, I know, my joy, they are saying that I am stealing wood, and they want to take me to court. They will soon bring a law-suit against the

Queen of Heaven herself!" ' That was not the only incident, and before long the ecclesiastical authorities made a fresh inquiry. Seven sisters were once working till nightfall near the Staretz' hermitage; they were about to take shelter in the hut which the father had built for them when three monks concerned with the inquiry arrived on the scene and began rummaging into all the corners. When they found nothing suspect they ordered the sisters to go home. The tales of these annoyances could be multiplied.

In the end Father Seraphim resolved to speak to those who were so spitefully accusing him: 'You see this great pine?' he said to them. 'I'm marking it with a cross. To prove to you that my dealings with the community of Diveyevo come not from my own will but out of obedience to the will of the Lord and his most holy Mother, we are going to ask this tree to fall towards Diveyevo.' The Staretz spent the whole night in prayer and so did the sisters. The next day, although there was not so much as a breeze, the huge tree was lying along the ground, uprooted; and the *Chronicles of Diveyevo* record many testimonies to this amazing fact. 'You who are accusing me,' the father then said to the monks who came along, 'look at this tree which testifies that my works are pleasing to God!' And the Staretz sawed up the tree and had it sent to the mill. For a long time its stump was preserved at Diveyevo in memory of this event.

## MANTUROV'S DEPARTURE

During this same year (1830) Manturov was to leave the holy Staretz. He departed to a distant province to manage the estates of a general who was away at the front during the Polish campaign. This officer had come to Sarov one day to thank Father Seraphim for his prayers during the Turkish war, and then returned another day to ask for his blessing. He met Manturov in the father's cell and was so taken with his open manner and noble, virile bearing that he offered him the post of estate-manager. To the amazement of them both, the Staretz raised no objection to his going but said to Manturov: 'Well, my joy, you're being sent away! There's nothing that can be done about it; it is the will of God. You have been faithful to me and you are going to miss me. But the General has to go and serve the Tsar and you will be in charge of his peasants who are forsaken and perishing in their poverty: they are getting involved in all kinds of sects, and you will be able to bring them back to our Church. It is because of this mission that I am letting you go.' Then he turned to Manturov's wife and said to her: 'And you, be a sensible woman; Michael has a fiery temperament which needs restraining. Don't let him get carried away, and let's hope he'll obey you!' Then they parted.

The Manturovs left for the district of Simbirsk, for the second time leaving a home that they had grown to love, and also the precious company of Father Seraphim whom they were never to see again. When they reached the Kuprianov lands they lost no time in carrying out the Staretz' instructions; the peasants, who had been completely neglected for years, found an upright man in Manturov and brought him their difficulties. He eased their lot and they were grateful to him.

Unfortunately the sojourn in that district had a bad effect on Manturov's health. He contracted malaria which was gaining many victims in the area, and wrote to his sister Helen, begging her to consult Father Seraphim as to what should be done about it. The Staretz gave Helen directions for medical treatment which Manturov used both for himself and for other patients, and many were cured. He regained sufficient strength to continue with his work.

Meanwhile the General, who had been so strongly attracted to him at their first meeting, never came to appreciate his devotion, as we shall see later, and when he had occasion to return to Sarov he sided with Ivan Tikhonovitch. The latter, taking advantage of his rival's absence, won Kuprianov to his cause and together they sowed great trouble at Diveyevo, obstructing the plans which Father Seraphim had made for the formation of the community and the construction of the cathedral.

## HELEN'S DEATH

After her brother's departure Helen took upon herself many of the responsibilites which had rested upon him; business correspondence, negotiations with civil and diocesan authorities, and the signing of contracts. She saw Father Seraphim's strength failing daily, and this grieved her deeply. She was sometimes heard to say: 'Our father will soon be leaving us, and I feel I can't live without him. If only I could die before he does!' She said this to the Staretz, who replied: 'Your maid, my joy, will go first, and she will take you with her.' Helen's maid, who had followed her 'young lady' was, indeed, suffering from lung trouble. Helen nursed her devotedly, but the girl was soon to die.

It was at that time that Helen received the disturbing news from her brother about his illness and she passed on his request for advice to the Staretz. Soon after this Father Seraphim sent for her and said: 'You have always obeyed me, my joy; well, now I want to give you an "obedience". Are you ready to fulfil it?' 'I'm always ready to obey you, father,' answered Helen. 'That's good, that's very good, my joy. . . . Now . . . you see, your brother is seriously ill, and he may possibly die . . . yes, he may die, but we cannot yet do without him . . . you understand this. So, this is your obedience: to die instead of your brother.' Helen answered quietly: 'With your blessing, Father.' And Father Seraphim began speaking about the mystery of death while Helen listened without saying a word. Suddenly she cried out: 'Father, I'm afraid of dying!' 'But what have we to fear from death,' replied the Father, 'it can only mean joy for us.'

Helen left the Father's cell, but hardly had she crossed the threshold before she fell in a faint in the arms of Xenia who was waiting outside the door. Father Seraphim told Xenia to lay her on the coffin which he had put ready for himself in his cell; he sprinkled her with holy water and gave her some to drink; then, when she went home, Helen went to bed, saying: 'I know I'm not going to recover.' A few days later she had to go and see the owner of the land on which Father Seraphim had planned to build the cathedral; the man agreed to sell it for 300 rubles. This was Helen's last obedience before she died.

According to a number of witnesses, her death was admirable. All fear vanished. Death meant to her the moment of giving her life for her beloved brother and for the community which was so dear to her. During her last days she seemed to be transported to another world: 'He is coming, He is coming!' she said, looking radiant, 'and the angels, the angels!' Xenia asked, in awe, 'My dear, do you see the Lord?' Helen's only reply was to sing in a weak, soft voice the hymn which she used to sing at funerals: 'No mortal can see the Lord's face, which even the angels dare not look upon. . . .' Xenia persisted, and then Helen answered quietly: 'Yes, Xenia, I've seen him as ineffable fire!' She had already received the Holy Sacraments; she then urged the sisters surrounding her to prepare her for burial. It was the vigil of Pentecost, 28 May 1832. Helen was twenty-seven. Her coffin was brought into the church while the bells began ringing for the Vespers of the feast. She was buried beside Mother Alexandra, near the spot where little Mary already lay. When the sisters came and told Father Seraphim the details of those painful hours he said to them: 'O how silly you are to mourn like this! If only you could have seen her soul! The cherubim and seraphim drew back when she went to meet the Holy Trinity!'

## MOTOVILOV

Meanwhile the Lord was going to bestow a great joy on his friend in the midst of so many grievous trials: this was the arrival of Nicholas Motovilov, to whom alone Seraphim gave the name, 'Friend of God'. At this time Nicholas was only twenty-two. His father, whom he lost in childhood, had at one time been a novice at Sarov, but he had gone back to the world and married. Before the birth of Nicholas he was told that his son would be one of God's elect.

Born on 3 May 1809, Nicholas inherited from his father large estates lying in three provinces of Central Russia. The management of these lands was a heavy burden on his mother and one day, when her son was seven years old, she decided to make a pilgrimage to Sarov. This was in 1816, at the time when Father Seraphim had just opened his cell door but was not yet receiving many visitors. The atmosphere in which he lived made a great impression on the child Nicholas, and a sketch of Seraphim's cell which he must have drawn at this time was found among his papers.

What particularly impressed the child was the large number of candles burning on seven stands before the icon of the Virgin of Tenderness. During his mother's conversation he began playing and jumping about between these candle stands; his mother stopped him but Father Seraphim told her: 'Just let the child play; his guardian angel is playing with him.' Then he said to Nicholas: 'Enjoy yourself, my boy, and may Christ be with you.' These words, so full of gentleness and kindness, Motovilov retained in his mind like a sweet song.

When he grew to adolescence he became interested in theology and often asked his professors embarrassing questions. He was particularly interested in the theology of the Trinity. It is said that at one time he even asked whether man, created in the likeness of God, might not also have a triune nature. Instead of interesting his masters, this kind of question only provoked their annoyance. 'You are trying to grasp what is beyond you!' they told him. His mother was also concerned about her son's future and his inquisitive spirit. She was even opposed to his going to a university, where liberal trends were asserting themselves. However she had to yield to Nicholas' desire, and he entered the University of Kazan. As his mother had foreseen, he was exceedingly disturbed and one day attempted to commit suicide. But then, on the edge of the lake, he had a vision of the Mother of God and an unseen hand held him back at the last moment. He discontinued his studies when he was only seventeen; his mother had just died, leaving him the care of his little sister.

Great trials were soon to come to him. He obtained an administrative post, but his honesty and ardent temperament gained him enemies among his superiors, and the spirit of the world bruised him so much that he fell ill. When remedies of all kind proved of no avail he decided to go on pilgrimage to Sarov.

'A year before he entrusted the community of Diveyevo to me,' he relates,[7] 'the great Staretz healed me of afflictions that paralysed and debilitated my body. I had been bedridden for three years, so my back was covered with very painful sores. On 5 September 1831 I arrived at Sarov; I had the joy of two conversations with Father Seraphim before being healed. On 9 September we set out for the hermitage near the spring. Four men were carrying me and a fifth supported my head. At the time the Staretz was sitting in a glade, talking to people. They seated me on a large felled pine beside the river. When I asked Father Seraphim to heal me he answered: "But I'm not a doctor; you ought to go to one of them." Then I told him all my troubles, the various treatments I had received without deriving any benefit. Finally I said that my only hope was in God's grace. The father asked me: "Do you believe in our Lord Jesus Christ who was made man, and in his most holy Mother Mary ever Virgin?" I said that I did. "Do you also believe", he went on, "that the Lord who used to heal solely by the power of his word can, in our days too, just as easily heal those who call on him? Do you also believe that the intercession of the Mother of God has an invincible power with her Son who can heal you?" I answered: "I believe with all my heart: indeed, without this faith I would not have had myself brought here!" "All right," he said, "if you believe, you are already healed." "How healed," I cried, "when my servants and you yourself are still holding me up?" "No, no," he answered, "you are now completely cured." And he told the men to step back; he took me by the shoulders, lifted me up and set me on my feet, and said, "Stand upright, plant your feet firmly on the ground! Don't be afraid!" Then he held my hand and gave me a slight push, and led me round the pine log. "See how well you can walk", he said. To which I replied, "But it's because you are holding me so well!" He withdrew his hand. "No," he said, "you can walk perfectly well without my help, because the Lord has healed you. Go on!" Then I felt a new power surging through me and I walked without fear. But Father Seraphim said to me, "That's enough for the present. Are you now convinced that the Lord has healed you and has forgiven your transgressions and pardoned your sins? Always believe in him, always trust in his great mercy, love him with all your heart and trust him utterly. Meanwhile," he continued, "do not abuse your power to walk, and preserve your health as a precious treasure sent by the Lord." He took leave of me, my servants went back by themselves, and I returned in the carriage to Sarov's guest house. The many pilgrims who had witnessed my cure told the story, and the news of the miracle preceded my return. When I arrived Abbot Niphont and the hiero-monks greeted me at the steps to the guest house and congratulated me on the grace which the Lord had vouchsafed to me. I must confess that I had never felt so well nor so strong as I did that day.'

Motovilov returned to Sarov as often as he could and one day the Staretz asked him point-blank: 'Friend of God, I feel you've a question to ask me. Don't be afraid to speak to unworthy Seraphim.' Nicholas then confessed that he was in love with a girl on a neighbouring estate and that he wanted to marry her. The Staretz seemed very interested in all that the young man told him, and from time to time asked some question about this girl; he asked how old she was. When Motovilov told him that she was seventeen, Father Seraphim answered: 'Friend of God, what are you telling me? She is only six and you will have to wait another ten years before you can marry her.' Taken aback and thinking that the Staretz had not understood him aright, Motovilov told him that the girl he was talking about was Catherine Yasykov and that she was old enough for him to marry her. 'But she is not the one I'm talking about,' said Father Seraphim, 'the fiancée destined for you by God is now only six years old.' Then he added, 'She is only a little peasant girl, but she is an angel of God.'

It was then four months to the day, since Father Seraphim had sent for little Helen, niece of the departed Mary, and had told the sisters who had brought her to bow to her, saying that she would become their guardian.

After a moment's silence the Staretz continued: 'There are two quite different things in life: one is when a man tries to order his destiny by himself, as you, friend of God, are now doing. The other is when the Lord himself disposes the destiny of someone whom he has chosen. . . .' And Father Seraphim bowed to Motovilov three times, saying: 'Promise me to do what I've just told you.'

## NOTES

[1] These words are from St Ephrem the Syrian.

[2] In making friends with the animals in this way Seraphim restored, as did some of the desert Fathers and St Francis of Assisi, the harmony with all creation.

[3] Cf. 'A hermit of the nineteenth century' in the *Moscow Journal*, 1903.

[4] These stories are preserved in the archives of Sarov and Diveyevo and some of them have been published in periodicals.

[5] Of petty bourgeois origin in Tambov, Ivan had had some artistic training and, at the age of eighteen, came to the monastery to enter the novitiate, but was not admitted at first. Ambitious and highly imaginative, he let himself be carried away by his fantasies. Through Father Seraphim's goodness he was eventually received, but he never

changed. Later, as we shall see, he was to be one of the chief causes of the Staretz' suffering.

[6] Owing to the multiplication of sects at this time, communities not registered by the state received no government subsidy and, in order to be recognized, had to obtain official status.

[7]Motovilov's Memoir, notebooks no. 40–60, *Chronicles of Diveyevo.*

# 7

# Towards the Summits

The trials of all kinds which beset Father Seraphim effected his transformation in Christ. He seemed to have passed beyond the frontiers of the visible world, and to have been freed from all earthly preoccupation. When he was forbidden to receive the Holy Gifts in his cell and had to go to the church to communicate, the pilgrims used to gather before the door of the infirmary chapel and wait for him to come out. They saw him coming by slowly, head bent, lost in God; then a little later he reappeared, clad in his white cassock, an inward brightness illuminating his face. His body seemed to have lost its material substance, so much so that it was sometimes literally snatched from the earth.

## LEVITATION
There is the witness of a young man who, smitten with paralysis, was brought to Sarov and introduced to the father by his aunt, Princess Chikaev. When the young man was brought into his cell the Staretz shut the door and told him to remain lying down relaxed while he himself went and prayed. He also told him to pray fervently himself, but without turning round. Then, forgetting the Staretz' order, the young man did turn round; he saw Seraphim raised from the ground. He cried out in astonishment and the Staretz, realizing that he had been found out, reproved the young invalid and enjoined him not to tell anyone what he had just seen. And, in actual fact, the young man did not reveal it until after Father Seraphim's death.

The same phenomenon manifested itself in the presence of four Diveyevo sisters. 'One day', says one of them, 'we were crossing a field and the grass was very high; Father Seraphim was walking ahead of us and enlarging on his subject. . . . He suddenly stood still and told us to go on ahead. We did what we were told but, inquisitive as we were, we turned round to look at him. We were dumbfounded; the Staretz was walking above the grass, lifted up from the earth. We threw ourselves at his feet while he himself was urging us: "O my joys, don't tell anyone about this as long as I am still alive!" '

Moreover the elements were submissive to him; water spouted up from the ground at his prayer, fire burst spontaneously into flame, animals in the forest obeyed his orders, and his very body lost its gravity. It seemed as though time and space no longer had any power over him; it was he who dominated them.

There was the time, for instance, that he was seen by the Diveyevo sisters beginning work on the moat while at the same time another sister saw him at his hermitage. There was also the rescue of a sister in distress, working at the mill. Another sister, afflicted with headaches, inwardly appealed to Father Seraphim to come and help her; she suddenly saw her cell lit up and the father came in to her and said: 'You called me, Mother, and I've come to console you.' With these words he raised her up, made the sign of the cross over her and departed. The headaches vanished immediately.

A little girl who was suffering from burns also saw Father Seraphim coming in to her room to ease her pain. When her parents later brought her to Sarov, what was her astonishment to recognize in the Staretz the 'little old man' who had come to comfort her. 'O, here's that little girl coming to see me!' exclaimed Seraphim, kissing her, just as though he too had recognized her.

During the cholera epidemic in 1831 Father Seraphim appeared to the wife of an officer, Teplov, and told her to draw water from the Virgin's Spring and give it to everyone in the area so that they might escape the sickness. The woman obeyed and even brought the water to the hospital where many sick people who drank it were cured.

Even today in Soviet Russia there are accounts of St Seraphim continuing to visit and console afflicted Christians.[1]

## THE MOTHER OF GOD

Further, we must consider Father Seraphim's astounding intimacy with the Mother of God.[2] He spoke of this to the sisters, to Manturov and to Father Vassili as something wholly natural. Such an intimate exchange existed between them that it found expression in his offering his closest friends mysterious fruits of strange flavour which the Virgin brought him when she came to see him. 'Ask me whatever you like, my friend,' the Mother of God had said to him. And more than any other gift Seraphim had implored her to protect his children.

So the Diveyevo sisters sometimes used to receive mysterious visits which they reported to the Staretz. Helen Manturov had seen a 'beautiful lady' in the church; another nun in the refectory, while she was working: 'Sitting in my corner, I hardly dared look at the beautiful lady who was attended by a young girl; thinking that Father Seraphim must have sent them, I felt embarrassed that no one was there to greet them. The lady went up to the table where I had prepared the bread for the following day; she took a piece, tasted it, and said: "It is good, this bread baked in obedience, prayer and with the Father's blessing." When the ladies left the room I hastened to give notice of their visit, but no one had seen them. The next day Father Seraphim sent for me and said: "Now, Mother, what about that Lady yesterday?" "Who was she?" I asked, "I didn't have time to greet her properly. . . ." But he, with a certain edge to his words: "What a great thing obedience is! It is better than prayer and fasting—she was the Queen of Heaven." '

As one reads the nuns' simple, artless tales in the

*Chronicles of Diveyevo* one receives the impression that for
Seraphim the frontiers between the visible and invisible
no longer existed.

Another sister, Eudoxia, tells how the father once talked
with the holy Mother of God.

'It was', she said, 'the vigil of the Feast of the Annunciation, 24 March 1831. The Staretz asked me to come to his
cell in the monastery, telling me that a great joy would be
granted me that day. We prayed together and then suddenly the father exclaimed: "Behold the Lord's grace coming down to us!" At that moment I heard a sound like a
soft breeze sighing through the tree tops, and then singing
swelled out. The air in the cell was laden with scent, rather
like incense but richer and sweeter. Then I saw Father
Seraphim prostrating and crying out in joy: "O most holy
Mother, O Virgin most pure, Queen full of grace!" And I
saw two angels coming forth, preceding the Queen of
Heaven. On either side of her were St John the Baptist and
St John the Apostle, and with them twelve virgin-martyrs,
each with a crown on her head. The whole cell was lit up
as though with the blaze of a thousand candles, and the
light went on increasing until it was brighter than the sun.
The walls seemed to expand and the cell to grow vast. Unable to bear such brilliance I fell senseless. Then I heard the
Queen of Heaven talking with Father Seraphim, but the
words, which seemed to come from afar, escaped me. The
only words I heard were: "Soon, my friend, you will be
with us!" She raised me up and invited me to speak to the
virgins, showing me each of them by name. Then the
Mother of God took leave of Father Seraphim and the vision
faded. . . . The Staretz told me later that it had lasted for
four hours. He said that he had entreated the Mother of
God to intercede with her Son not only for the sisters of
the community but also for all those who loved him, worked
for him, and followed his counsels.'[3]

This vision might be interpreted as that of the praying
Church as represented on the icon *Deisis* (supplication or

intercession): towards Christ in majesty, seated on his glorious throne, converges the prayer of his Mother with those of St John the Baptist, of the Bridegroom's beloved disciple, and of the whole company of angels and apostles. A few months before he died it was granted to Father Seraphim to have this vision of the Church Triumphant which he was soon to join.

## CONVERSATION ABOUT THE HOLY SPIRIT

Even more impressive was Father Seraphim's intimacy with the Holy Spirit. He was clothed in and lived by this blessed Presence which made him an authentic 'bearer of the Spirit'. What he was able to say about it, or, rather, to reveal to Motovilov, is now well known, but it bears repeating.

In November 1831, a month after Father Seraphim's conversation with this young man concerning his future, the Staretz sent for him again. One of the Diveyevo sisters came to find him in Sarov's church where he was praying in his usual place before the icon of the Virgin. 'Are you the lame young man whom the father healed?' she asked him. When he said he was, she told him that the Staretz was asking for him and was waiting for him in his cell in the monastery.

'Those who have been to see him at Sarov or who have heard people talking about him can imagine how my heart overflowed with joy at this unexpected summons,' wrote Motovilov. 'So, leaving the church, I hastened to him. At the doorway to his cell Father Seraphim said to me: "I want to see you, friend of God, because I've much to tell you, but first let me finish with my orphans." He gave me a stool by the stove and went back to his cell. Two hours later he said goodbye to the sisters and said to me: "I've kept you waiting, friend of God. It couldn't be helped: my orphans needed consoling. But come in now." He spoke about various matters concerning the salvation of my soul and then told me to come again the next day, with the

guest-master, to his Near Hermitage. Father Gury[4] and I
spent the whole night talking, without being able to sleep for
sheer joy and, the next day, fasting, we set out for the
Near Hermitage. There were others coming to the hermitage and the Staretz had not yet opened his door. "There'll be
a long wait," Father Gury said to me, "the horse is hungry
and we may be attacked by wild beasts from the forest."
"Go back by yourself if you're afraid," I answered. "I'm
staying here." In actual fact Father Seraphim very soon
opened the door and said to me, "I did tell you to come,
friend of God, but it's Wednesday today, a silent day: so
make it tomorrow, but have breakfast first." Then, turning
to Father Gury, he said: "And you, my friend, tomorrow
bring this young man to the glade. Go in peace!"

'Words cannot express the joy that welled up. Although
I was still fasting and had waited a whole day I felt abun-
dantly reassured and refreshed. To anyone who has not
experienced the delight and fulfilment that come to a man
on whom the Spirit of God rests, my words may seem empty
and my story fantastic; however, I testify that everything
I am going to state is the pure truth without any exag-
geration and that it is only a very faint reproduction of
what I felt.

'So it was Thursday; it was a grey day and the ground
was covered with a thick layer of snow. Great flakes were
still falling when Father Seraphim began talking to me in
the glade close by his Near Hermitage, on the banks of the
Sarovka. He seated me on a recently-felled tree-trunk and
sat down opposite me.

' "The Lord has shown me," he said, "that when you
were a child you wanted to know the goal of the Christian
life and that you had put this question to a number of
eminent ecclesiastics." I must confess that this question
had indeed weighed heavily on my mind since I was
twelve, and that I had often asked it without receiving a
satisfactory reply.

' "Yet no one," continued Father Seraphim, "told you

anything definite. They instructed you to go to church, to pray, to do good works, telling you that there lay the goal of the Christian life. Some of them even said to you: 'Don't search into things that are beyond you.' Well, miserable servant of God that I am, I am going to try to explain to you what this goal is. Prayer, fasting, works of mercy—all this is very good, but it represents only the means, not the end of the Christian life. The true end is the acquisition of the Holy Spirit."

' "What do you mean by acquisition?" I asked the father, "I don't quite understand."

' "To acquire means to gain possession," he replied. "You know what it means to earn money, don't you? Well, it is the same with the Holy Spirit. The aim of some men is to grow rich, to receive honours and distinctions. The Holy Spirit himself is also capital, but eternal capital. Our Lord compares our life to trading and the works of this life to buying: 'Buy from me gold . . . that you may be rich' (Rev. 3. 18). 'Make the most of the time, because the days are evil' (Eph. 5. 16). The only valuables on earth are good works done for Christ: these win us the grace of the Holy Spirit. No good works can bring us the fruits of the Holy Spirit unless they are done for love of Christ. That is why the Lord himself said, 'He who does not gather with me, scatters.'

' "In the parable of the virgins, it was said to the foolish virgins when they had no oil: 'Go to the dealers and buy.' But while they went, the door to the marriage feast was shut and they couldn't get in (cf. Matt. 25. 9–13). The lack of oil is usually interpreted as the lack of good works, but this is not the real meaning. What good works could be termed lacking when, although the maidens were called foolish, they had preserved their virginity? Virginity is one of the greatest virtues, a state which we call angelic and which could include all virtues. Unworthy as I am, I dare to think that what they were lacking was the grace of the Holy Spirit. For the essential thing is not just to do good but to

85

acquire the Holy Spirit as the one eternal treasure which will never pass away. Yes, this oil that they lacked symbolizes the grace of the Holy Spirit, the fruit of all virtues, without which there can be no salvation. Indeed, is it not written: 'Through the Holy Spirit is every soul exalted in purity, and illumined by the Triune Unity in mystic holiness'?[5]

' "This Holy Spirit, the All-powerful, is given to us on condition that we ourselves know how to acquire him. He takes up his abode in us and prepares in our souls and bodies a dwelling-place for the Father, according to the word of God: 'I will live in them and move among them, and I will be their God and they shall be my people' (2 Cor. 6. 16).

' "Among works done for the love of Christ, prayer is the one that most readily obtains the grace of the Holy Spirit, because it is always at hand. It may happen that you want to go to church but there isn't one nearby; or else you want to help a poor man but haven't anything to give or you don't come across one; or yet again you may want to remain chaste but natural weakness prevents your resisting temptation. But prayer is within reach of all men and they can all give themselves to it, rich and poor, learned and unlearned, strong and weak, the sick and the healthy, the sinner and the righteous. Its power is immense; prayer, more than anything else, brings us the grace of the Holy Spirit."

' "But Father," I said, "you are only talking about prayer; tell me about other good works done in the name of Christ."

' "Yes," replied Father Seraphim, "you can obtain the grace of the Holy Spirit by means of other good works. Put capital in the bank of heaven and see what interest will accrue to you. So, if prayer and vigils bring you divine grace, watch and pray; if fasting brings it, do penance; if it comes from almsgiving, then give alms. As you know, I come from a merchant family in Kursk; well, when I was still in the world my brother and I did our trading and

86

always bought and sold those wares which brought us most profit. Do the same yourself because, for us Christians, the meaning of life doesn't consist in increasing the number of good works but in deriving the greatest profit from them, by which I mean the more excellent gifts of the Holy Spirit. And you in turn must be a distributor of this grace, like a lighted candle that shines and gives light to other candles without extinguishing its own flame. If earthly fire is like this, how will it be with the fire of the Holy Spirit? Earthly goods disappear when they are given away, whereas the riches of divine grace go on increasing in those who distribute them. So our Lord said to the Samaritan woman: 'Everyone who drinks of this water will thirst again, but whoever drinks of the water that I shall give him will never thirst: the water that I shall give him will become in him a spring of water welling up to eternal life' (John 4. 13–14)."

' "Father," I said again, "you keep on saying that the grace of the Holy Spirit is the goal of the Christian life, but how or where can I see such a grace? Good works are visible, but can the Holy Spirit be seen? How can I know whether or not he is in me?"

' "In our days," answered the Staretz, "owing to the tepidity of our faith and to the lack of attention we give to God's intervention in our life, we are completely estranged from life in Christ. That is why the words from the Bible seem so odd to us, such as, 'Adam saw God walking in the garden' (Gen. 3. 8) or those in the Acts, where it is said that the Holy Spirit, after preventing Paul the Apostle from going into Bithynia, sent him to Macedonia (Acts 16. 6–10). Many other passages from scripture tell us of God's appearing to men. Some people say that these texts are incomprehensible, or else they deny that man can see God with the eyes of the flesh. This incomprehension is due to the fact that we have lost the simplicity of the early Christians and, with our so-called enlightenment, we plunge ourselves into such dark ignorance that what was easily understood by the ancients escapes us. (I am referring to their understanding of God's appearances.) Thus it is said of Abraham and of Jacob that they saw God and spoke with him and that Jacob even wrestled with him. Moses also gazed on him, and so did all the people with him, in that pillar of cloud which was none other than the grace of the Holy Spirit acting as a guide to the people of Israel in the wilderness. God, the grace of the Holy Spirit, was not seen in a dream or ecstasy, nor only in the imagination, but in reality and in very truth. Because we have become careless over the work of our salvation we no longer grasp the meaning of God's words as we should; we don't pursue grace and our pride doesn't give it a chance to take root in our souls. Neither have we that light of our Lord which he bestows on those who long for it with fervour and hunger and thirst.

' "When our Lord Jesus Christ, after his resurrection, vouchsafed to complete the work of our salvation, he sent to his apostles that breath of life which Adam lost, and he gave the grace of the Holy Spirit back to them. On the day of Pentecost he bestowed on them the power of the Holy Spirit which entered them in the form of a mighty wind and in the appearance of tongues of fire, filling them with the strength of his grace. This light-filled breath, received by the faithful on the day of their baptism, is sealed by the rite of chrism on the members of their body so that it becomes a vessel of grace. That is why the priest accompanies the anointing of the chrism with these words: 'The seal of the gift of the Holy Spirit'. This grace is so great, so necessary and life-giving, that it is never withdrawn: even the lapsed retain it until death. Thus we know that if we did not sin after baptism we should remain holy, free from every taint of body and soul, like God's righteous ones. The tragedy is that as we grow older we don't go on growing in grace and intelligence but, on the contrary, by our mounting perversity we separate ourselves from the grace of the Holy Spirit and become great sinners. But, the wonder is that Wisdom is ever seeking our salvation. If at her entreaties man listens to her voice and resolves for love of her to be vigilant, if he gives himself to good works and attains true repentance, then the Holy Spirit acts in him and builds in him the kingdom of God.

' "The grace of the Holy Spirit, given at baptism in the name of the Father, and of the Son, and of the Holy Spirit, continues to shine in our heart as divine light in spite of our falls and the darkness of our soul. It is this grace that cries in us to the Father: 'Abba, Father!', and who reclothes the soul in the incorruptible garment woven for us by the Holy Spirit.

' "To give you more light on this subject, friend of God, I must tell you that the Lord often revealed the workings of this grace in those whom he sanctified and illumined. Remember Moses after his conversation with God on Mount Sinai: the people could not look at him because of the dazzling light that shone from his face and he could only be with them when he covered it with a veil (Ex. 34. 30–35). And recall our Lord's transfiguration as well: 'His face shone like the sun, and his garments became white as light' and 'the disciples fell on their faces and were filled with awe' (Matt. 17. 2 and 6). When Moses and Elijah appeared illumined by this light we are told that a cloud came and covered the disciples with its shade to enable them to bear the brightness of that divine grace which blinded their eyes. Well, it is by this ineffable light that the action of the grace of the Holy Spirit manifests itself to all those to whom God vouchsafes to reveal it."

' "But how", I asked him, "can I know that I am within this grace of the Holy Spirit?"

' "It is very easy, friend of God," replied Father Seraphim, "because everything is easy to those who have obtained understanding. It is our misfortune that we don't seek after the Wisdom that comes from God. The apostles, having acquired this Wisdom, always knew whether or not the Spirit of God rested in them; when they possessed it they were sure that their work was holy and acceptable to God.

89

With this basic certainty they were able to write in their letters: 'It seemed good to the Holy Spirit and to us' (Acts 15. 28) as being a statement of the unshakeable truth necessary to the faithful. So you see, friend of God, it is very easy!"

'Then I answered, "I don't quite grasp how it is possible to be absolutely sure of living in God's Spirit. How can it be proved?"

'The Staretz reiterated: "Friend of God, I've already told you that it's very easy: I've told you that some men found themselves filled with the Holy Spirit and were able to be convinced of his presence; what more do you want?"

' "How I long to understand completely!"

'Then Father Seraphim gripped me firmly by the shoulders and said: "My friend, both of us, at this moment, are in the Holy Spirit, you and I. Why won't you look at me?"

' "I can't look at you, Father, because the light flashing from your eyes and face is brighter than the sun and I'm dazzled!"

' "Don't be afraid, friend of God, you yourself are shining just like I am; you too are now in the fullness of the grace of the Holy Spirit, otherwise you wouldn't be able to see me as you do."

'And, leaning towards me, Father Seraphim said quietly: "Thank the Lord for his ineffable goodness: you may have noticed that I didn't even make the sign of the cross; only in my heart I said this prayer to the Lord: 'Lord, grant him the grace of seeing clearly, with the eyes of the flesh, that outpouring of your Spirit which you vouchsafe to your servants when you condescend to reveal yourself to them in the reflection of your glory.' My friend, the Lord granted it instantly—merely at poor Seraphim's prayer. How we must thank him for this gladness that he has given us both! As a mother comforts her children, so does he fill our penitent hearts. So, my friend, why not look at me? Come on, look, don't be afraid, for the Lord is with us!"

'Then I looked at the Staretz and was panic-stricken. Picture, in the sun's orb, in the most dazzling brightness of its noon-day shining, the face of a man who is talking to you. You see his lips moving, the expression in his eyes, you hear his voice, you feel his arms round your shoulders, and yet you see neither his arms, nor his body, nor his face, you lose all sense of yourself, you can see only the blinding light which spreads everywhere, lighting up the layer of snow covering the glade, and igniting the flakes that are falling on us both like white powder.

' "What do you feel?" asked Father Seraphim.

' "An amazing well-being!" I replied.

' "But what exactly is it?"

' "I feel a great calm in my soul, a peace which no words can express."

' "This is the peace, friend of God, which the Lord promised to his disciples when he said: 'Peace I leave with you, my peace I give to you; not as the world gives do I give to you' (John 14. 27). It is that peace which the Apostle calls 'the peace which passes all understanding' (Phil. 4. 7). This is what is filling your heart now. And what else do you feel?"

' "A strange, unknown delight."

' " Yes, that's how it is with those delights which the Psalmist describes, saying that the sons of men will be given drink from the river of God's delights and will feast on the abundance of God's house (Ps. 36. 8). These delights fill us with an ineffable blessedness that melts our heart, a blessedness that is beyond words. What more do you feel?"

' "An amazing happiness fills my heart."

'Father Seraphim went on: "When the Holy Spirit descends and fills the soul with the plenitude of his presence, then we experience that joy which Christ described, the joy which the world cannot take away. However, the joy you now feel in your heart is nothing compared to that which Paul the Apostle describes: 'What no eye has seen, nor ear heard, nor the heart of man conceived, what God has prepared for those who love him' (1 Cor. 2. 9). The first fruits of that joy are already given us and if our soul is even now filled with such glad sweetness, what words can express the joy laid up in heaven for those who sorrow here below? And you too, friend of God, have had grief in your life; see how joyfully God has already comforted you in this world. Do you feel anything else, my friend?''

' "I'm amazingly warm."

' "Warm? What are you saying, my friend? We are in the depths of the forest, in mid-winter, the snow lies under our feet and is settling on our clothes. How can you be warm?''

' "It's the warmth one feels in a hot bath."

' "Does it smell like that?''

' "Oh no, nothing on earth can be compared to this! There's no scent in all the world like this one!''

' "I know," said Father Seraphim, smiling, "It's the same with me. I'm only questioning you to find out what you're discovering. It is indeed true, friend of God, that no scent on earth can be compared with this fragrance, because it comes from the Holy Spirit. By the way, you've just told me that you've been feeling the warmth of a hot bath, but look: the snow settling on us isn't melting, neither on you nor on me. That shows that the warmth isn't in the air but is within us. This is what the Holy Spirit causes us to ask God for when we cry to him: 'Kindle in us the fire of the Holy Spirit!' Warmed by it, hermits are not afraid of winter hardship, protected as they are by the mantle of grace which the Holy Spirit has woven for them. This is as it should be, for divine grace comes to live in our hearts, within us. Didn't the Lord say: 'The kingdom of God is within you' (Luke 17. 21)? This kingdom is just the grace of the Holy Spirit, living in us, warming us, enlightening us, filling the air with his scent, delighting us with his fragrance and rejoicing our hearts with an ineffable gladness. At this moment we are with those whom the Lord mentions as not tasting death before they see the kingdom of God come with power (Luke 9. 27; Mark 9. 1). Now you know, my friend, what it's like to be in the fullness of the Holy Spirit, as Macarius the Great writes: 'It was as though I were engulfed in the outpouring of the Holy Spirit.' This is what we are filled with today, in spite of our unworthiness. Friend of God, I don't think you'll ask again how to recognize the presence of the Holy Spirit. Treasure this memory of the revelation given you of the fathomless loving-kindness of God who has visited you today."

' "Father," I replied, "I'm not sure that the Lord will enable me to keep the remembrance of his mercy vivid for ever; I'm so unworthy."

' "I'm quite sure," the father replied, "that God will help you to remember these moments for ever, otherwise in his goodness he would not have been so swift to answer poor Seraphim's prayer. Besides, this revelation hasn't been given you just for your own sake but, through you, to the whole world, so that, confirmed by the action of grace, you may use it in serving your neighbour.

' "The fact that I am a monk and you a layman doesn't make any difference. What counts in God's eyes is true faith in him and in his only Son. It is for this that the grace of the Holy Spirit is given us; the Lord seeks hearts overflowing with love for him and their neighbour, and this is the throne where he would sit and reveal himself in the fullness of his glory. 'My son, give me your heart', he says (Prov. 23. 26). For in the heart he builds the kingdom of God.

' "Well then, friend of God, now that you've had the privilege of the favour just granted to you, tell it to all men seeking salvation. 'The harvest is plentiful, but the labourers are few' (Matt. 9. 37; Luke 10. 2). We are called to God's work, and he has sent us gifts of grace so that we can do it. By helping our neighbour to enter the kingdom we bring God the fruits we have harvested. So let us follow the example of those faithful servants who brought their master a double yield of what they had received.

' "The Lord is near to all who are faithful to him and

who love him with their whole heart. He answers a layman's prayer just as he does a monk's, provided they are both living in faith, even if this faith is no bigger than a grain of mustard seed. Yes, he enables them both to move mountains, because 'all things are possible to him who believes' (Mark 9. 23). Thus it is, friend of God, that you will be able to obtain from God everything that you ask him, whether it is for his glory or for your neighbour's benefit. Besides, you know well that whatever you ask for the benefit of others redounds to his glory, as he himself has said: 'As you did it to one of the least of these my brethren, you did it to me' (Matt. 25. 40).

' "And now I have told you everything, I have shown you what the Lord, through the mediation of poor Seraphim, has vouchsafed to reveal to you; go in peace, and may the Lord and his most holy Mother be with you now and always and from all ages to all ages."'

'From the instant when Father Seraphim's face became filled with light, the vision did not fade; the Staretz remained in the same position that he was in at the beginning of the conversation and this ineffable light went on shining all the time he was talking.

'I am prepared to take an oath on the truth of my words.'[6]

That is the account of one of the great episodes in the life of Father Seraphim and it is the most important message he has left us: the efficacy of baptism which makes it possible for us to be born and to live in the Spirit. This same doctrine is likewise to be found in St Gregory of Sinai (1255–1346). For him the spiritual life consists in rediscovering baptismal energy and in seeing its light. Prayer is the shortest way to attain this. Such a discovery results in a sense of plenitude and fervour which gladdens the spirit and consumes the soul with ineffable love for God and men. And St Symeon the New Theologian considers the effects of baptism to be real indeed when its grace really makes the conscience aware of the presence of the Holy

Spirit in the soul and enables it to see the light of God's glory.[7] He describes, under a pseudonym, a vision that came to him one night when he was praying and invoking the Name of Jesus: 'A brilliant divine radiance descended on him from above and filled all the room . . . he became wholly dissolved in this divine light and it seemed to him that he became light, and he forgot the whole world. . . .'[8]

However, that ecstasy received by St Symeon differs from the phenomenon described by Motovilov in the sense that neither he nor the Staretz seem to have been in a state of rapture, since they were both aware of their surroundings. The significance of what happened to Father Seraphim might be summed up in the words of St Paul: 'If any one is in Christ, he is a new creation; the former being has passed away, a new being is born' (2 Cor. 5. 17). God's presence among men and in them, revealed on the day of Pentecost through the descent of the Holy Spirit, manifests itself daily in human life in Christ. When the Staretz urged Motovilov to keep the memory of this event alive and fresh he sent him into the world to bear witness to this 'new life' vouchsafed to men in the Holy Spirit. It is noticeable that Father Seraphim's words are wholly based on the classical exegesis of the biblical passages which he cites. In the interpretation of the parable of the ten virgins he seems to follow the thought of St Macarius in his fourth homily; he sees the oil for the lamps as the grace of the Holy Spirit which the foolish virgins lacked. St Macarius explains that this grace makes it possible for human nature to overcome the grossness of the flesh, to regenerate it and surpass its limits in that quest for the treasure beyond price which is the love of the Holy Spirit. Father Seraphim likewise follows St Macarius in the figure of trading, the symbol of the human soul that has to gain its heavenly heritage by earthly means.'[9]

This event in the life of St Seraphim has been studied and commented on right up to our own days and it never

ceases to make one marvel at the wonderful things which
the Lord accomplishes in those who love him.

## MOTOVILOV'S DEPARTURE

Motovilov spent eight months at Sarov working on the
administration of the Diveyevo community under Father
Seraphim's direction. Thanks to his care the little community of the Mill increased to several acres of cornfields.
Motovilov had a house built for himself in the village of
Diveyevo and he very often went from there to the
Staretz' Near Hermitage to talk over the work with him.
A great friendship united them. This very intelligent young
man with his rare spirituality gave himself to the Staretz
wholeheartedly and used to call himself 'Seraphim's
humble servant'. One day Father Seraphim sent for him
and spoke to him at great length about all Diveyevo's concerns; he explained the smallest details, initiated him into
all the plans which had not yet materialized and declared
that he, Motovilov, was the man who had been chosen by
the Mother of God as the community's future foster father.
Therefore it would fall to him to take up this work when
he (Father Seraphim) would no longer be in the world.
Then he sent for two sisters who, later on, were to play an
important part in the monastery's life through their witness. Taking their right hands, he put them in Motovilov's,
by this act conferring on him the future of the community.
'From now on you must bring all problems to him, without
hiding anything,' he said. Then, turning to Motovilov, he
continued: 'A day will come when you and Michenka
(Manturov) will be the only witnesses of what has been
done at Diveyevo.'

Just as Abbot Pakhomius on his death-bed had entrusted
the care of the Diveyevo sisters to his spiritual son Seraphim, so he in his turn entrusted his 'little orphans' to the
care of his devoted disciple Motovilov. This man, who was
neither monk nor cleric, by this solemn act took over the
work to which Seraphim had dedicated the greater part of

his life. When the time came for Motovilov to return to his official duties, the father allowed him to go.

Motovilov was to return to Sarov once more before the Staretz died: during the summer of 1832 he was again smitten with severe illness. Father Seraphim spoke to him about his restoration to health and reminded him that his 'fiancée' was waiting for him at Diveyevo. He also spoke of events that were to overtake Russia but, alas, Motovilov was unable to carry out his intention of publishing the prophecies of the man of God.[10] Then the Staretz told him that this time poor Seraphim would not be the one to work his cure, but that Archbishop Anthony of Voronezh, to whom he was to go immediately, would do so, for such was God's will. The father knew that his end was very near; he entrusted his friend, the friend of God, to this holy man who would henceforth direct his life. Seraphim gave Motovilov his blessing, and then they separated. Neither Manturov nor Motovilov was to see their spiritual father again in this life. Father Seraphim was now entering into final solitude of spirit, set free from all earthly bonds.

God alone was his country.

## NOTES

[1] Cf. Father Vladimir Rodzianko's talk at the Holy Spirit Conference, Royal Foundation of St Katharine, 1972, recorded on Gustaf Weigel Society tape.

[2] The Orthodox Church's veneration for the Mother of God is inseparable from its devotion to Christ. She is the 'Theotikos', the Mother of God, forming an inseparable part of the salvation mystery and a figure of the Church. Her power of intercession with her divine Son places her at the head of the company of the saints. She is Jacob's ladder leading to the heavenly dwelling places and is the link between the present world and eternity.

[3] The phenomena of a supernatural order which one observes in the lives of the mystics may be compared to Christ's parables. One needs 'eyes to see' and 'ears to hear' and this is granted only to the

poor and to the pure in heart. It does not pertain to rational conjecture; it surpasses this.

⁴ Father Gury, later Abbot George, published his memoirs of Father Seraphim at St Petersburg in 1845.

⁵ Antiphon of Sunday Matins.

⁶ For more than seventy years after Father Seraphim's death, Motovilov's manuscript remained buried under a pile of old documents in a grange at Diveyevo. It was through the efforts of the writer S. A. Nilus that it could be deciphered. He came to Sarov in May 1903 and was greeted by Motovilov's widow, the former little Helen, then seventy-seven years old and still living at Diveyevo. She also handed over to the writer all her husband's archives. When he came across the text of the conversation he made no delay in getting it published in the *Moscow Gazette* during that same year 1903 in which Seraphim had just been canonized.

⁷ Cf. *Writings from the Philokalia on Prayer of the Heart*, pp. 143–152.

⁸ The phenomena of divine light were known since the first centuries of Christianity by the desert fathers. They affirmed that the purity of the human spirit enables the light of the Holy Trinity to shine in man who, in turn, sheds it abroad. There is also St Benedict's vision, cited by Gregory Palamas: 'He saw the whole universe gathered together in one ray of light.' In his work, *Participation in God*, Palamas writes: 'The saints do not merely participate in God; he gives himself to them. Not only do they themselves enjoy God's presence, but this presence manifests itself through them to others. . . . They do not merely live, they vivify.' Palamas defines the divine light as the result of deification, thanks to which 'God shines forth through the mediation of the body and soul of those who are deemed worthy.' 'The saints', he says, 'constitute the substance which the fire of his grace consumes.' Cf. John Meyendorf in *A Study of Gregory Palamas* tr. George Lawrence (London 1964), p. 208.

⁹ The style of Motovilov's manuscript gives the impression that these notes were made soon after the conversation took place, because they preserve Father Seraphim's manner and way of speaking and recall a number of details which it would have been difficult to remember after a lapse of time. One might add that the manuscript, published by Nilus, aroused a great polemic in the papers and that the writer had to defend himself against a number of attacks originating from members of the Synod. He also published the details of this controversy in his book, the Russian title of which was *Velikoye v Malom* which might be translated 'The greatness of the seemingly insignificant'. It is now recognized that these matchless pages of

manuscript contain one of the great moments in the history of Christian mysticism.

[10] Nilus was able to decipher some of these prophecies concerning the trials which Christians would have to endure before the coming of the Lord: 'In those days', the Staretz said, 'Christians will know something of the Son's experience when he cried to his Father, "My God, my God, why hast thou forsaken me?" This sense of being abandoned by God will have to be endured by Christians, though only for a short time, after which the Lord will come in all his glory and will accomplish to the full those things which God in his divine counsel decreed.'

# 8

# Instructions and Final Teaching

Father Seraphim did not write much; he spoke to a few people, monks, nuns, and lay folk when there was need for it, and about the things of God to his Diveyevo orphans and to his friends. Hieromonk Gury, who was a friend of Motovilov, took what notes he could of the words he heard from the Staretz, but it must be recognized that what we learn from him and Hieromonk Sergius who was later to edit these notes is only a minute part of what Saint Seraphim used to share with others concerning God's marvels. These *Instructions* of Father Seraphim give indisputable evidence of his knowledge of the *Philokalia* and the whole Hesychast tradition; but above all they are the echo of personal experience, of a life with Christ in the Holy Spirit. Manifestly it is this which gives them their interest. When Hieromonk Sergius gave them to Philaret, Metropolitan of Moscow, with a view to publication, censorship[1] was rather severe, which it had every right to be because of the personal character of Seraphim's words. 'He does not speak like other people.' In the eyes of the ecclesiastical authorities the *Instructions* seemed to introduce a certain novelty into doctrine; this, unfortunately, was because these men had succumbed to the western fault of scholasticism and had lost the vital sense of life in Christ. The *Instructions* did get published in 1839 as an appendix to the life of Mark the Hermit. They were reprinted in 1841 but were altered by Metropolitan Philaret who wrote to Anthony of Voronezh: 'I have taken the liberty of correcting certain passages which are expressed in an unusual way, in order to avoid

misunderstanding.'[2] Undoubtedly this is most unfortun-
ate!

From the very first paragraph these notes introduce us
to God's world: 'God is a fire,' the fire of which Jesus spoke
when he said: 'I came to cast fire upon the earth; and
would that it were already kindled!'[3]

*God is a fire.* He warms the heart and inward parts. When
we feel a chill in our hearts coming from the devil (for the
devil is cold) let us call on the Lord. He will come and
warm us with perfect love, not only love for himself but
for our neighbour as well; and at the touch of this fire
Satan's chill will vanish.

*On the knowledge of God.* To the degree that a man purifies
himself before God and walks in his presence, God will show
him his face even in this world. The saints gazed at (contemplated) his image as in a mirror.

If you have not yet come to know God it is impossible to
love him, if you cannot love him it is because you have not
contemplated him. It is the knowledge of God which enables
us to see him, because contemplation comes only with
knowledge.

*On loving God.* Whoever knows perfect love for God lives
in this world as though he were not in it and regards himself as a stranger and sojourner on earth, because he sees
nothing but God alone. He is wholly transformed in love
for God and has no other affection. When the moment
comes to leave the body the soul who is filled with divine
love has no fear of the prince of this world but flies as it
were from a foreign land to her native country, escorted by
the angels.

*On faith.* Whoever possesses true faith is a cornerstone in
the temple of God, chosen for the work of God the Father,
raised up by the power of Jesus Christ with the help of the
grace of the Holy Spirit.

'Faith apart from works is dead' (James 2. 26). Now the

works of faith are: love, peace, patience, mercy, humility, tranquillity, acceptance of the cross, life in union with the Holy Spirit. True faith cannot exist without good works: whoever believes always does what is good.

*On hope.* All those who live through strong hope in God are raised up to him and illumined by the brightness of eternal light. True hope seeks only the kingdom of God, knowing that everything needful in this life will be given to it.

Man's heart will never be at peace until it has found this hope.

*On the fear of God.* A man deciding to follow the way of inward contemplation must, before all, be inspired with the fear of God; this is the beginning of wisdom (Prov. 1. 7); without it he may lay himself open to the words of the Prophet: 'Cursed is he who does the work of the Lord with slackness' (Jer. 48. 10). So let him go forward with extreme prudence and most profound respect for all that is holy!

*On gifts received.* A man must make every effort to keep inward guard over the spiritual treasure of gifts already received, otherwise he may lose them without ever being able to retrieve them. That is why he must never, except in case of necessity, reveal the secrets of the heart to others. However, if necessity demands and the right moment comes, he may reveal them for the glory of God.

*On vain talking.* Nothing so much as idle words has power to extinguish that fire brought by Christ and enkindled in man's heart by the Holy Spirit.

*On Prayer.* According to Isaac of Syria: 'Prayer without distraction is that which produces constant thought of God in the soul.' It is through prayer that God unites himself with our souls and dwells in us. St Symeon the New Theologian has explained the method of prayer excellently in the *Philokalia* and St John Chrysostom has magnificently extolled prayer's worth. All those resolving to serve God must persevere in prayer, saying inwardly: 'Lord Jesus Christ, Son of God, have mercy on me a sinner.' One may likewise turn to the protection of the Mother of God, asking her help and addressing her in the words of the archangel's salutation.

When mind and heart are united in prayer and the soul is wholly concentrated in a single desire for God, then the heart grows warm and the light of Christ begins to shine and fills the inward man with peace and joy.

*On tears.* All the saints and monks who withdrew from the world shed tears in hope of eternal consolation. . . . We too should weep and ask remission of our sins. St Isaac again counsels us: 'May the tears of your eyes water your face, and the grace of the Holy Spirit rest on you and purify you from all stain. The heart of the weeping man is lit by the light of the Sun of Righteousness, Christ, who said to us: "Blessed are those who weep, for they shall be comforted." '

*On despondency.* Despondency is a worm gnawing the heart. Anyone resolved to fight his passions must also contend with despondency. Just as a pale complexion betrays sickness, so despondency reveals someone still involved with his passions. He who has renounced worldly things is always happy.

*On sickness.* God in his loving-kindness sometimes allows the body to be tried by sickness: this is so that a man's passions may lose their force.

*On patience and humility.* We should bear trouble patiently because our life lasts only a moment in comparison with eternity. Insults too, should be borne patiently and you should take your wounded heart to God alone.

Plunge yourself into humility and 'you will see the glory of God', St Isaac of Syria tells us.

*On almsgiving.* 'Let a merry heart precede the gift you give' is again St Isaac's teaching.

103

*On love of neighbour.* We must be gentle with our brother and encourage him with a loving word when we see him getting into trouble. We should never judge him, even if we have seen him committing a fault, because we do not know how often we ourselves will be enabled to preserve purity of soul. 'If you see your brother committing a fault', says St Isaac again, 'cast your cloak over it.'

*On the necessary care to be had for the soul and its provisioning.* We should take the greatest care of our soul; as for the body, we must look after it proportionately as it serves the soul well. If we exhaust our body to the point of also exhausting our spirit, we are like madmen, even though we are behaving in this way for the sake of overcoming the passions.

The soul must be provisioned with the divine Word, and specially given to reading the New Testament and the Psalms. Their light illumines the spirit and man is transfigured by this light. It is best to devote oneself to this reading in solitude; read the whole Bible attentively. Then God fills one with his grace and bestows the gift of understanding. When a man is nourished on this Word he receives the divine fire and the gift of tears.

*On inward peace.* There is nothing better than peace in Christ, for it brings victory over all the evil spirits on earth and in the air. When peace dwells in a man's heart it enables him to contemplate the grace of the Holy Spirit from within. He who dwells in peace collects spiritual gifts as it were with a scoop, and he sheds the light of knowledge on others. All our thoughts, all our desires, all our efforts, and all our actions should make us say constantly with the Church: 'O Lord, give us peace!' When a man lives in peace, God reveals mysteries to him.

*On guarding the heart.* One must constantly watch over the heart. The heart cannot live unless it is full of that living water which boils in the heat of the divine fire. Without that water the heart grows cold and becomes like an icicle.

*On the signs of divine grace.* When a man becomes the object of divine grace he has no need of an outward sign: the fact that he possesses this gift convinces him that it comes from God, because he tastes its spiritual fruits: love, joy, peace, patience, kindness, goodness, faithfulness, gentleness, self-control (Gal. 5. 22–3). But when Satan assumes the likeness of an angel of light, or even uses good means, one is aware of it in one's heart by reason of a certain anxiety of thought and a sense of worry. St Macarius explains this precisely when he says: 'Satan always betrays his presence by some sign.' And St Gregory of Sinai takes up the same thought, saying: 'You can always discern whether the light you see in your soul comes from God or Satan by the effect it has on you.'[4]

*On contrition.* St Boniface tells us that the fear of God always begets attention; and attention, interior peace which awakens the soul's conscience. The work of conscience consists in showing the soul its shortcomings as though reflected in clear, translucent water. Thus contrition is born.

*On the light of Christ.* To receive and be aware of the light of Christ within one, it is necessary to withdraw from outward things, as far as this can be done. After purifying his soul by contrition and good works and proclaiming his faith in Christ crucified, a man should shut his eyes and concentrate on bringing his mind down into the depths of his heart, ardently calling on the Name of our Lord Jesus Christ. Then according to the measure of his desire and the ardour of his heart for the Beloved, he will find a sweetness in the invocation of the Name that provokes a longing to seek the supreme illumination. When the mind is concentrated in the heart through this exercise, then the light of Christ begins to shine, lighting up the temple of the soul with its divine radiance. This light, according to St John the Evangelist, is the life of men (John 1. 4). When a man contemplates this eternal light within him his mind remains pure and detached from every carnal image. Lost in

105

contemplation of the uncreated Beauty, he forgets everything sensory, he even forgets himself, and would prefer to
be buried in the heart of the earth rather than lose his
unique treasure—God.

*On the active and contemplative life.* The spiritual life must
be approached with inward fear and trembling, with
humility and contrition, and after long study of the holy
scriptures. It would be preferable, at the beginning, to be
directed, to find an experienced staretz; if this is impossible
one must try to go forward helped by the Word of God.

Two stages are to be noted in the spiritual life: the active
life and the contemplative life. The first consists in renun-
ciation and ascetic effort: the second is the goal.

The active life consists in fastings, abstinence, vigils, pros-
trations, and other exercises which help one to progress in
the narrow way that leads to eternal life.

Since man possesses both body and soul, his life is of
necessity both corporeal and spiritual, action and contemplation.

Man's activity enables him to purify his passions and,
when he has freed himself from all stain, he can then draw
near, very humbly, to the contemplative life.

This consists in raising the mind towards the Lord God
in 'pure prayer', as St Isaac of Syria calls it, in watchfulness
of heart, in spiritual recollection.

The practice of the active life is not to be laid aside when
one has attained to the lofty heights of the contemplative
life; on the contrary, it has to be strengthened.

Everyone wishing to progress in the spiritual life has to
ascend the ladder of perfection rung by rung, occupying
himself first in the practical labours of the active life and
gradually ascending towards the heights of contemplation.[5]

Such were the great themes of teaching which the
Staretz gave to monks, to his orphans, and to the crowds
who never ceased to besiege him right up to the last day of
his life which, as it happened, was not far away.

## LAST COUNSELS

Father Seraphim's strength was failing daily, yet he never uttered a word of complaint. 'My life is drawing to a close,' was all he said, 'but if my body seems already dead, my spirit makes me feel like a new-born child.'

When the Diveyevo sisters came to find him he said to them: 'You'll have to live by yourselves from now on, because I shall be leaving you.' But the sisters did not know that he was telling them about his death. They thought he was wanting to go and live as a recluse again.

The Mother Superior Parascovia came one day to find him in his Near Hermitage. The Staretz sat on a tree-trunk and the mother knelt beside him. Then Father Seraphim opened the New Testament which he always carried about with him and began to read the chapters of St John about Jesus' last discourse with his apostles. He ended with these words of the Lord: 'Truly, truly, I say to you, if you ask anything of the Father, he will give it to you in my name. Hitherto you have asked nothing in my name; ask, and you will receive, that your joy may be full' (John 16. 23). 'What joy, what bliss will fill the soul,' he said, 'when the Lord's angels come and fetch it to bring it into his presence!'

He began making his final preparations. For instance he wrote and asked certain people to come and see him for the last time; to others he had already said goodbye. 'We shall not meet again,' he said to visitors who were intending to come back to Sarov; while to those who insisted: 'My door will be shut.' He hardly ever went to his 'desert' any more, and received fewer callers. He was often to be seen sitting on his coffin, deep in thought.

However, he continued to look after his orphans and, when he was strong enough to go into the forest, he sent for them one by one to give them various counsels. The road from Diveyevo to the forest lay through Sarov; as the sisters went on their way they sometimes caught up with the Staretz, walking very slowly, bent double and leaning on his pick or the handle of his axe. When the Sarov monks saw the sisters making this trek of nearly 25 kilometres they were sorry for them and invited them in winter to call at the monastery guest house on their way back, to rest and get warm. 'The old man makes you go all that way,' they said to them, 'he makes you shiver with cold and he hasn't much to give you in return.' Father Seraphim warned them not to listen to the monks and he strictly forbade them to stop at Sarov, except in the church if it was time for the Liturgy. Some of them, influenced by the monks, began to murmur and even thought of going home to their villages; however, the Staretz knew how to calm their troubled hearts and give them fresh courage.

Father Seraphim increasingly withdrew from the monastery's external rites and customs. He was even wont to assume those mysterious ways known as 'folly in Christ', sometimes in his appearance, sometimes in his words, the meaning of which did not become known until later. Sometimes he was seen to be exposed to the stings of flies and mosquitoes without taking any notice of them. When someone wanted to drive them away he said good-naturedly: 'Let them be, we ought not to kill what God has created, because "everything that has breath praises the Lord".' He used to dress rather oddly and when anyone remarked on it he answered: 'There was a prince who thought the rags given him by a beggar far more beautiful than the purple and ermine robe which he had previously worn.'

When he was utterly worn out by all the people he retired to his cell, intending to sleep, but even when he had shut himself in he had no rest, for people came and knocked on the door and persisted until he gave in. Sometimes he hid himself in the forest, covered by dead leaves and branches. That was how a young man found him. This youth had come to ask him about his vocation before leaving the world and becoming a monk. He found Father Seraphim under a tree, hidden by the tall undergrowth and seemingly asleep. Clad in a simple peasant smock, girded with a cord with a bag of bread tied to it, the Staretz looked like a shepherd. Such simplicity and humility so impressed the young man that it determined his monastic future far more than words could have done.

In July 1832 Father Seraphim healed a sister and when she said on leaving that she looked forward to seeing him again, the Staretz' answer was to raise his hands towards heaven: 'We shall meet up there.'

He also healed a little girl of four who had gone blind; he bathed her eyes with water from the spring and told her mother to pray. On the following day the girl was healed.[6]

During the month of August, Arsenes, Archbishop of Tambov and future Metropolitan of Kiev, came to Sarov. After he had inspected the monastery he asked to be taken to Father Seraphim, who was at the spring at the time.

'What are you doing, Elder of God?' asked the Archbishop.

'I'm strengthening the bank with stones so that it won't be washed away by the flow,' answered the Staretz.

'Very good, very good,' replied the prelate, 'but would you permit me to see your "little desert"—in the midst of the desert?'

So the father brought him to his hut and gave him a rosary, a packet of candles wrapped in a cloth, a pair of woollen stockings and a bottle of oil for lamps. The Archbishop was moved by this presentation and asked: 'But I believe you have an even more remote hiding-place in your desert?' and without waiting for the Staretz' reply he went towards the stove behind which (he had been told) there was an alcove. 'You'll get dirty,' Father Seraphim warned him, but the Archbishop had already opened the little door leading to a hiding-place so small that it was very difficult to get in. There, too, was an icon of the Mother of God with a lamp before it. The Staretz used to go down there to pray, to escape being pestered by people who were incessantly knocking on his door.

On leaving the Staretz, the Archbishop advised him not to give pilgrims wine, but only to give them pieces of blessed bread. The Staretz bowed to the ground and promised to follow his advice. The next morning before dawn, when he went to Matins, he passed the rooms where the Archbishop was staying; he requested that he should return the bottle of red wine which Seraphim had, on the previous day, given to him with his other gifts.

A letter from the Archbishop, preserved in the monastery's archives, gives the meaning of these gifts of the Staretz: the candles, oil and wine which he had preserved intact until Seraphim's death were used for his memorial liturgy; but the Archbishop kept the stockings, cloth and rosary as precious souvenirs of the gracious welcome he had received from the man of God. He also understood the symbolic meaning of the work the Staretz was doing at the spring when he met him there. He once explained in a letter: 'The Staretz is dead; but as for me, I have to go on, with God's help, strengthening the Church's banks so that the flood-water does not inundate her.'

There is also a story that when some merchants from Kursk came to visit the holy man and brought him a message from his brother, he simply said to them: 'Tell him that I am praying for him.' We know that his brother died soon after he himself had gone to God.

Nearly all the Diveyevo sisters had treasured memories of their last talks with the Staretz, most of which were later to find a place in the monastery's *Chronicles*.

Sister Matrona relates that once when she came to the Staretz' hut the bells began ringing for Matins. 'You hear the bells ringing,' the father said to her, 'so go along quickly.' And he sent her away. As she was going she turned round and was astounded to see the Staretz standing by the door, shining with light. She took several steps and turned round again. He was still surrounded with light. When she stopped for the third time she saw the Staretz bowing to the ground to her. It was the last time she saw him in this world and she realized later that his gesture had been his way of saying goodbye.

Father Seraphim confided to Mother Eudoxia: 'When Antichrist comes he will have no power over you. You yourselves may not see him, but others will live till then and witness this event.' 'What troubles there will be when Antichrist starts snatching crosses from the churches! Many will then forsake these places. . . .

'If you see these things, don't be upset by what is flying through the sky or floating on the sea. Get your sack and your boots ready, one pair to wear and another spare one!' Was he speaking of coming wars? Did he foresee the great Revolution and the emigration of the White Russians?

At the beginning of December 1832 the Staretz said to Sister Dorothea: 'Do you know what darnel is like, my joy? Well, take heed of these words: when all the darnel among you has been pulled up, you will see Diveyevo's crop growing up tall, green and beautiful. Be sure to remember what I am telling you.' He was silent for a moment and then he continued: 'Goodbye, my joy! I have committed you all to the Holy Virgin, Joy of all joys. The time will come when many people will want to call themselves your "father", but don't let yourselves be persuaded by what they say. Ivan Tikhonovitch too will style himself your "father" but it is I alone, poor Seraphim, who have begotten you all.'

Another time Father Seraphim sent for Father Vassili Sadovski and told him: 'After your wife's death it will be your turn to die; well, when the time comes for you to go to God, ask to be buried by the Church of the Nativity, you on the right and Michenka[7] on the left. How good it will be to rest in peace! And I, in the middle of you! Thus we shall all be together!' Then Father Seraphim took off his cuffs and put them on Father Vassili's wrists, to signify that he was transferring to him the care of his sheep.

All through the years when the father was looking after the community he used to provide for the sisters' needs, so much so that a few days before he died he sent for two of them and gave them a bag of money, telling them to buy

111

everything needed for a year, even advising them what purchases to make.

'When I am no longer with you', he told them, 'come to my tomb often, bring all your worries, all your troubles, tell me everything that is grieving you, talk to me as to a living person because, for you, I shall go on living; I shall listen to you and your sorrow will disappear.'

He used to compare human life to a lighted candle: 'The wax symbolizes faith; the wick, hope; and the flame is love which joins all together.' He used to leave candles burning before the icon even when he was not there. His neighbour, Brother Paul, often told him that it was dangerous not to put them out, but the Staretz answered: 'So long as I am alive there will not be a fire; only when I die will fire announce my death.'

Knowing this habit of his, monks in adjacent cells sometimes used to come and ask for a light. So it came about one night that a monk was surprised to see the father's cell plunged in darkness. 'O dear, the lamp has gone out,' said the Staretz, 'however, it must go on burning for a bit longer.' And while Father Seraphim was saying this the monk saw a little glimmer appear in front of the icon; it soon grew to a thread of bluish light curling itself round the wick in the lamp which lit up at the same instant. Father Seraphim then took a candle, lit it from the lamp and, holding it in his hand, told the monk to blow on the flame. The candle went out. 'So will my life go out very soon,' he told him; and as he said these words his face reflected so bright a light that the monk prostrated himself on the ground, seized with fear and grief at the warning of the Staretz' death. Father Seraphim lifted him up, saying: 'O my joy, this isn't a time for grief: it is a time to rejoice at the great happiness to come.'

## LAST DAYS

On Christmas Day that year he communicated as usual in the infirmary church; then after the liturgy he had a long conversation with Abbot Niphont, with whom he interceded on behalf of the young monks. On returning to his cell he picked up a little icon of the Appearing of the Holy Virgin to St Sergius of Radonezh and said to a monk who was there: 'Lay this icon on me when I die and bury me with it; Archimandrite Anthony sent it to me after blessing it on St Sergius' relics.'

On New Year's Eve Father Seraphim went to put a stone by the apse of the cathedral of the Dormition to mark the spot where he wanted to be buried.

The next day, Sunday, he went to the infirmary church and put candles before the icons; and he kissed them all as a sign of farewell. The Liturgy had not yet begun and the church was in pitch darkness. The Staretz sat down on a bench and Ivan Tikhonovitch, who was going to conduct the choir, came up to him. The father gave him his blessing, reminding him of the advice which he had already given him, and read him a passage from the first chapter of St Peter on the approach of the Parousia (the return of Christ in glory) and the behaviour of Christians in the world (1 Peter 4. 7–15). It is known, through the monks of Sarov, that Ivan did not understand the Staretz' warning and interpreted it, in accordance with his own ideas, as the father's blessing on the realization of his plans.[8]

During the course of that day the Staretz' neighbour, Brother Paul, heard him singing the Easter hymns: 'We have seen Christ's resurrection, let us worship the Lord Jesus!' 'Shine, shine, New Jerusalem, for the glory of the Lord has risen upon you!' 'O Passover, great and most holy, O Christ, O Wisdom, Word, and Power of God! Grant that we may more perfectly partake of you in the day that knows no end, in your Kingdom!'

The next day at dawn Brother Paul left his cell to go to Matins; as he went past Father Seraphim's door he smelled smoke. He knocked but received no answer. He went quickly to tell the monks who were making their way to the church in the early dawn. They thought at first that Father

Seraphim had gone to the forest without putting out his candles and that a fire must have started in his cell. A novice burst open the door. It was pitch dark inside, and full of smoke. They ran to fetch a candle, and brought snow, and then saw Father Seraphim in his white cassock, kneeling before the icon of the Virgin of Tenderness. On the lectern pages of the Gospels were smouldering; the monks concluded that sparks must have fallen on them from the candle Father Seraphim had been holding while praying. The monks thought he had dropped off to sleep from weariness, because his body was still warm. They tried to wake him, but in vain. His heart had stopped beating.

The news was brought to Abbot Niphont; it spread through the monastery. After the traditional ablution of the dead, Father Seraphim was clothed in his monastic habit and brought in his coffin to the cathedral of the Dormition. So that as many people as possible could bid him farewell and assist at his funeral, Father Seraphim's coffin remained open for eight days. Thousands of people came from all parts to kiss the Staretz for the last time. There was such a crush in the cathedral that the candles went out for lack of air.

It is related that at the hour of Father Seraphim's death an extraordinary light lit up the sky and that a monk in the vicinity of Kursk, seeing it, said to a novice who was with him: 'It is the soul of Father Seraphim flying to heaven.'

NOTES

[1] Censorship was instituted in the Russian Orthodox Church during the reign of Nicholas I (1825–1855).

[2] Letter of Philaret, Metropolitan of Moscow.

[3] The desert fathers experienced the kindling of this fire; they said, for instance, through the mouth of Abba Joseph: 'You too can become wholly fire.' Cf. *Paradise of the Fathers* (London, Chatto & Windus 1907), vol. 2, p. 68.

[4] The Fathers said a good deal about that 'discernment of spirits' without which one cannot walk in the truth of Christ.

## Instructions and Final Teaching

⁵ The arrangement of paragraphs in the *Instructions* is not the same in different biographies of St Seraphim; there are also a number of variants in the text. We ourselves have preferred to include the Staretz' teaching on silence, solitude, and the ascetic life, for example, in the body of the narrative.

⁶ When such people found the father at the spring he would give them its water to drink, and he used to send it to those who were unable to come there. So bottles of water began to travel throughout all Russia. The Staretz readily bathed sick limbs in this water, drying them with a towel with which he was always girded. This was the origin of the custom of sending him pieces of linen and woven and embroidered cloths, as a token of thanks.

⁷ Michael Manturov.

⁸ The interpretation he gives to this episode is described in the biography of Father Seraphim which he published in St Petersburg in 1849 and which was reprinted several times during the nineteenth century.

# 9

# Diveyevo after the Staretz' death

## THE STARETZ' SPIRITUAL PRESENCE

After the Staretz' death the 'orphans' of Diveyevo put
themselves under the care of Father Vassili Sadovski. They
often gathered together before the icon of the Virgin, 'Joy
of all joys', which, at Abbot Niphont's order, was brought
from Father Seraphim's cell to the community refectory.
Thus the Staretz' prophecy was fulfilled, for he had said
that one day the refectory would become the dwelling place
of the Queen of Heaven. Moreover, the father's unseen
presence was felt in the smallest details of the sisters' life;
in all their difficulties they turned to him for spiritual help.
Every evening they gathered together round a candle and,
each in turn, recounted this or that detail of the Staretz'
life which had especially struck them. Thus, little by little,
those stories were born which, together with several other
later testimonies, made up the *Chronicles of Diveyevo*. During those evenings Father Seraphim seemed to join their
circle and fill their hearts with joy and comfort. This
presence sometimes became really tangible, when the father
actually appeared to them.

Thus, two years after his death, on New Year's Eve 1835,
he revealed himself to one of the sisters. She felt an urge
to go to the church, and there she saw Father Seraphim,
wearing glistening white vestments and coming to meet
her.

'Is it you, Little Father?' cried the sister.

'Of course it is, my joy, don't you recognize me? Yet
you go on calling me. O how unbelieving you are! Don't

116

you realize by now that I'm celebrating with you in the church every day?' And with these words he returned to the sanctuary through the Royal Doors.

There were many instances of Father Seraphim's appearing to people at Diveyevo who had never seen him, especially to save them from some danger threatening their life. Legends grew up that ran from mouth to mouth. One of them tells the story of the merchant who, one winter night, was travelling by *troika* along the Diveyevo road. He was caught in a blizzard; snow flakes whirled around in the gusts of wind making it impossible for him to find the road. Half-frozen, he sent up a prayer to Father Seraphim; immediately he heard someone walking beside him. 'Follow me,' said an unfamiliar voice. He soon made out an old man and an old woman going on ahead of him, drawing a small sleigh which left clear tracks in the snow. The man followed the tracks; when he deviated to right or left the voice called out: 'Not this way, not that way, just follow me!' Even at full gallop the merchant's horses could not catch up with the mysterious sleigh: nothing but the tracks left in the snow and the voice that went on helping him. Hardly were the horses back on the road again before the lights of the village were seen in the distance. The old people and the tracks vanished. The merchant arrived safe and sound at the village inn. Overcome, he realized that this little old man and that old woman were none other than Father Seraphim and Mother Alexandra who had answered his call for help.

THE FALSE DISCIPLE

Meanwhile, at Diveyevo, the difficulties which had begun during the Staretz' lifetime went on increasing, for lack of competent direction. 'When I am gone', Father Seraphim had said, 'you will no longer have either father or mother!' These words became a fact. Mother Parascovia had resigned, because at her age the direction of a community then numbering over 300 religious was too much for her. After her, five superiors succeeded one another in a few years; death carried off two of them, and the others confessed themselves incapable of ruling. Things came to such a pass that, in 1842, Ivan Tikhonovitch had no difficulty in obtaining permission to amalgamate the community of the Mill with that of Mother Alexandra under the direction of a single superior, Mother Irene. She was a daughter of old Mother Xenia and had been brought up at the convent since early childhood; with a weak and pliant disposition she was unable to withstand the influence of Ivan who had installed himself in the convent in spite of the sisters' protests. He wrote to St Petersburg describing the position of the two communities in a very arbitrary way and asking the ecclesiastical authorities to amalgamate them. This was done by order of the Holy Synod. The event caused consternation in the community and even sowed discord among the religious. As soon as the request for amalgamation was granted Ivan sent one of the sisters to St Petersburg to collect alms. The first subscribers were the Tsarina, the Grand Duke (heir to the throne), and the Grand Duchesses. This response indicates the influence of the 'painter of Tambov'[1] at the Court, but without a doubt it was really Father Seraphim's name that touched the hearts of the august donors.

Ivan Tikhonovitch used the proceeds of the collection to build a church according to his taste. Father Seraphim's churches were closed; Mother Irene raised no objections and gave way to the orders of Father Seraphim's false disciple, who succeeded in winning over even the Archbishop of Tambov. Most of the buildings erected by Father Seraphim were demolished and a group of new ones rose in their place. Ivan planned to level the Virgin's Moat. The monks of Sarov, in spite of their suspicions, did not openly oppose these changes, seeing that they had little interest in the works of the man of God. It must be admitted that the memory of the Staretz won least respect among the monks. 'Diveyevo is where he has the greater veneration,' they said, 'as for us, we are still waiting for some marvel before we believe in him.' However, there were tales of strange happenings there; for example, the light that was sometimes seen on the Staretz' tomb, or again, appearances, miracles. But a monk is a man slow to believe.

Ivan finally decided to build a cathedral at Diveyevo. We know how dear this project had been to Father Seraphim's heart. But Ivan's plan was drawn up according to his own ideas and not according to the father's; he wanted to build on a distant site, some kilometres from Diveyevo in the direction of Sarov, and he was intending to transfer the community itself to the same place. It was at this poignant moment that Michael Manturov, Father Seraphim's true disciple, appeared on the scene as the father's own envoy.[2]

When Father Seraphim died, Manturov, who was still on General Kuprionov's estates, did not know about it for some time, because of the difficulties of communicating with that distant province. When he went to Sarov after the Polish campaign the General heard of Father Seraphim's death before Manturov did. Ivan took advantage of his arrival to sow doubts about Manturov whom he accused of dishonest intentions towards the Staretz. It is to be remembered that Manturov did, in fact, have all the papers concerning the purchase of the land belonging to the community. The father had told him to keep them in his possession, no doubt foreseeing the treachery of his false disciple Ivan.

In his conversation with the General, Ivan persuaded him that Manturov was insisting on keeping all the documents for the purpose of influencing Diveyevo's future affairs. He well knew that after the father's death Manturov would oppose his intentions. So he resorted to a wicked plot, begging the General to persuade Manturov either to hand over the papers or, better still, to sell the land himself. The General, who had little business experience and was all too credulous, believed everything that Ivan Tikhonovitch told him. But the only answer he received from Manturov was: 'You can kill me, if you like, but I'm not parting with those papers at any price. I'm beginning to understand why the Staretz entrusted them to me.'

Angry at Manturov's obstinacy, the General dismissed him, without even rewarding him for his three years' service.[3] And so it came about that Manturov, now penniless, undertook the journey back to Diveyevo with his wife. A long and difficult journey! Tramping along the dusty roads, for food they had to be content with whatever good people gave them out of pity. One day in Moscow when Manturov was praying before the icon of the Virgin of Iverskaya, a stranger gave him some rubles and disappeared. With that money they were able to continue their journey, and when they arrived at Diveyevo they were welcomed by Father Vassili.

Manturov's wife, since the day when, as a young girl, she had come to share her husband's life at Diveyevo, had become his great help-mate; she had attained ardent faith in God's will and was profoundly devoted to Father Seraphim. Moreover, as we read in her memoirs, preserved in the *Chronicles of Diveyevo*: 'Once when I was still rebellious Father Seraphim gently handed me a book on the Lives of the Saints, pointed to a page about a martyr, and told me to read it carefully. Without knowing Slavonic, to my astonishment I began to decipher the text and, as I went on, the meaning of what I read unfolded before my eyes. After that I found that I knew Slavonic without ever having learned it.' That martyr's passion was as it were a presage to Anna Manturov of what she and her husband would have to endure at Diveyevo.

Michael Manturov was distressed to see what was happening to the community but he could do nothing because, now that he was reduced to poverty, his influence was almost non-existent. The opposition he sometimes raised to Ivan Tikhonovitch's illicit actions increased the latter's hostility. Indeed, his attempts to carry out Father Seraphim's wishes nearly cost him his life; for one day his enemies set fire to his house, and the little he had went up in flames. Fortunately some people devoted to the Staretz' memory helped him build another home, opposite the church, where he lived to the end of his days.

The site on which Ivan Tikhonovitch was intending to build the cathedral was a disused quarry where tunnels had been made to a depth of twenty metres. In spite of opposition from the architects and other knowledgeable people, Ivan told the workmen to begin digging the foundations, and he invited Archbishop Jacob of Nijni-Novgorod to come and bless the work on 14 June 1848.

When the Archbishop arrived Manturov immediately laid before him all that he knew about Father Seraphim's plans; he told him how Father Seraphim had sent his sister Helen to buy the land which he himself had chosen. Thoroughly upset, the Archbishop went to the site where Ivan and the workmen were waiting. A crowd of nearly 4,000 people from the surrounding district had gathered there, having heard that the Archbishop was coming, and they were eagerly awaiting the event which had caused a great stir in the neighbourhood.

It was getting dark, though it was still possible for the Archbishop to distinguish the remains of the former quarrying. The agitation increased; muttering was heard, and unflattering remarks about Ivan Tikhonovitch—'Let's wait and see Father Seraphim bringing his cathedral back to its proper place!' Then, to everyone's delight, the Archbishop pronounced: 'May the Lord bless this foundation on the spot which Father Seraphim foresaw and which Michael Manturov has shown me;' and then he continued, 'but how can we start digging again on another site, with the civil dignitaries coming tomorrow to take part in the ceremony?' 'There are plenty of us and we'll get it done,' the men cried out, and at once, led by Manturov, the people made their way to the site that he had shown to the Archbishop and set to work. With the help of the neighbouring peasants, the workmen toiled all night and the foundation ceremony was able to take place on the following day, on the spot that Father Seraphim had indicated.

While this was happening Ivan, beside himself, asked to be transferred to another monastery in the jurisdiction of Nijni-Novgorod.[4]

Unfortunately ten years later, in 1858, the cathedral was still not built as Ivan Tikhonovitch persisted in his opposition. Manturov was deeply grieved at this state of affairs and, although he was not ill, he was preparing for death.

'I'm coming to fetch you', Father Seraphim told him in a vision. Then, on 7 July 1858, after he had made his Communion, he came out of the church and collapsed on a bench. His hour had come to enter the Kingdom.

## THE ROLE OF THE FOSTER FATHER

There still remained 'Seraphim's humble servant' Motovilov, who was also absent at the time of the Staretz' passing. Father Seraphim sent him, it will be remembered, to Archbishop Anthony at Voronezh, in whom he found a spiritual father and friend. His host kept him there after his cure, and Motovilov spent quiet, happy days working in the Archbishop's library on the life of Mitrophan of Voronezh whose canonization was in process. However, towards the end of December 1832 he suddenly became anxious and consumed with a burning longing to see the Staretz. Archbishop Anthony, who also saw into the future, refused to let him go; he foresaw what a shock the news of the Staretz' death would be to Motovilov. So, on the morning of 2 January 1833 Motovilov, stirred by a misgiving, burst into the Archbishop's room. Without giving him time to speak the Archbishop told him that during the night, at about 2 o'clock, an old man had come to see him and had told him, weeping, that he was grieving for a friend whom he was leaving behind on earth. Hearing this, Motovilov exclaimed: 'Don't hide the truth from me but have mercy on me: that soul, it was mine, a sinful soul weeping for his Staretz who has gone away to his Lord. O tell me, Father,

122

this old man is Father Seraphim, and he is dead, isn't he?'
'Yes,' replied the Archbishop, 'Father Seraphim died last
night.' 'Then why did you keep me here when I wanted to
go to Sarov?' 'Because you would have found him dead
when you arrived. You can't get to Sarov from Voronezh
in three days!' 'Well, I'm going at once!' cried Motovilov.
'God bless you,' said the Archbishop. During that same day
of 2 January, without waiting for the official notice of Father
Seraphim's death, Archbishop Anthony publicly announced
the sad news and had solemn prayers said for the soul of the
venerable deceased.

Motovilov left immediately and arrived at Sarov on
11 January, two days after Father Seraphim's burial. Seeing
him so heartbroken, Abbot Niphont gave him the Bible
which the Staretz used to read every day; its pages bore
traces of the fire on the night of his death. Motovilov
eagerly collected all the mementoes of his friend. He even
bought the two huts of the Near and Far Hermitages and
had them transported to Diveyevo where they were made
into chapels.

Soon afterwards he travelled to Kursk to glean some information about the Staretz' childhood and youth, but the
results were scanty. For the Staretz' brother had died a few
days after he did, as Father Seraphim had predicted; the
house where his parents had lived was no longer there,
having been demolished to widen the road. Only one witness, an old man who lived nearby, recalled that he had
known the young Prokhor; he it was who told Motovilov
the few facts which we know concerning the Staretz' childhood. On his return to Sarov Motovilov entrusted these facts
to Ivan Tikhonovitch, for at this time he thought he was
a true friend. Ivan used them later when he wrote the
biography of Father Seraphim which was published in
1849. However, the journey to Kursk had very dreadful
repercussions. As he himself relates in his memoirs,[5] the
devil wanted to wreak vengeance on the work which
Motovilov had undertaken in order to make the Staretz

known. He relates how, on the return journey as he reread
the notes he had made, he was seized by doubts. How was
it possible for the devil to afflict men of such consummate
holiness as Father Seraphim with such terrible tempta-
tions? All this seemed inconceivable to him. While he was
thinking about it he felt a freezing, noisome cloud envelop-
ing and saturating him, paralysing his limbs and preventing him from making the sign of the cross. 'The tortures
that the devil inflicted on me were infernal,' he wrote.
These attacks recurred for a period of about thirty years.
But Father Seraphim, who had been given a revelation of
his friend's whole life, once said to him: 'If the Lord himself
had not shown me, I would hardly have believed it possible
for souls as complicated as yours to exist on earth. Your
whole life, friend of God, will be strewn with strange, fantastic events, for the simple reason that the carnal in you
is so mixed up with the spiritual that it is hard to separate
them. . . . But in the end, after a troubled life, the Lord will
grant you a peaceful death in Christ. 'What will my life
be?' asked Motovilov. 'The Lord has forbidden me to show
you,' replied the Staretz. 'I can only tell you this: when you
are blamed, bless God; when you are persecuted, be at
peace; and when men speak evil of you, let your heart
rejoice! This is the road you and I have to follow here below.'
That was the last talk which Motovilov had with the
Staretz. On his first visit, Seraphim had seen Motovilov's
angel playing with him; now he saw the devil coming to
this rare soul. That was why before he died he sent him
to Archbishop Anthony, so that he would have a father and
friend who was a saint.

Although he decided to dedicate his life to the holy
Mother of God, Motovilov was unable to resist the bonds
which tied him to the world; he had always loved the young
Yazykova, but she gave him a flat refusal which grieved
him deeply. A little later she was to marry the famous
writer, theologian and philosopher Khomiakov, who owed
much of his sensitive loftiness of soul to her. So Motovilov

waited for the fiancée whom the Staretz had promised, and he lived a life full of contradictions: he loved society, yet at the same time he could live for months without leaving Diveyevo, only going to church; he loved long pilgrimages on foot, and at the same time was given to mad runs in the *troika*. The world thought him a fool, while Russia's two great men of God at that time, Father Seraphim and Archbishop Anthony, chose him as friend and confidant.

One spring when he found himself at Sarov he suddenly felt driven by an irresistible urge to return to Voronezh in order to spend Easter night with Archbishop Anthony. The ice on the lakes and rivers had not yet melted and Motovilov hoped to be able to cross them by sleigh without mishap. 'You know my horses,' he said to Abbot Niphont, who was warning him against the journey. Indeed the stud on his estate at Simbirsk was famed throughout Russia and he had even been privileged to offer a very fine team of horses to Tsar Nicholas. Motovilov left on Easter Eve; when he was only fifty kilometres from Voronezh he stopped in a village and the peasants warned him that the neighbouring locks were about to be opened and that the spring waters would start flowing and would break the ice. Motovilov was too impatient to make a detour and the arrow-like *troika* shot towards the opposite bank. The sleigh was barely halfway across when the sluice gates were opened and the flood surged over Motovilov, engulfing him and his *troika* too. He came to himself on the opposite bank; the horses and driver were safe and sound. They tipped the water out of the sleigh and, 'Drive on!' cried Motovilov. He arrived just in time for the Easter Liturgy. Archbishop Anthony was leaving his rooms to go to the church. 'Saint Mitrophan of Voronezh told me you'd arrived;' he said to Motovilov, 'go and get changed quickly and come, we'll give thanks to the Lord.' Motovilov's valise and its contents had remained intact, without letting in a single drop of water.

That Easter Liturgy remained engraved on his memory

for the rest of his life, so sublime was its vision. Motovilov saw the Archbishop surrounded by light and, when he uttered the words of the eucharistic canon, tongues of fire leapt from his mouth and rested on the celebrants and faithful. However, this divine fire did not remain on all who were assisting. Some became light, others coal black. Two or three times during the Office the Archbishop gave Motovilov a penetrating glance which seemed to ask: 'Do you see these manifestations of divine grace?' To which Motovilov gave an answering glance: 'Yes, I see them and I rejoice exceedingly.' After the holy liturgy the two mystics spent the whole night talking about God's mysteries revealed to men here below, and the bonds of friendship which already united them were strengthened yet more.

In 1840 Motovilov spent a whole year at Diveyevo and made the acquaintance of that fiancée mysteriously predestined by the Staretz. She was a girl of seventeen whose beauty and modesty smote Motovilov's heart. He married her soon after. Helen Meliukov, young Mary's niece, was a peasant, a fact which displeased many. The couple lived on the estate at Simbirsk but often returned to Diveyevo, spending long holidays at the house which Motovilov had built there. The community of sisters benefited greatly from this, for Motovilov always acted as its foster father.

When, in 1840, the two communities amalgamated, Motovilov, enlightened by Manturov, at last comprehended Ivan Tikhonovitch's nefarious role. He even declared one day: 'If I had been there the situation would never have developed. I regard the day of the amalgamation as utterly disastrous, for I can now see in all its loathsomeness the infidelity to the Saint's wishes.'

Meanwhile Ivan (now known as Joasaph) was informed of his victory. He spent his time in propaganda for his own cause, both at St Petersburg and among the sisters, urging the election of a new superior of his own choosing after the resignation of the previous one. He set his choice on a novice, Sister Glykeria, who was a peasant but had some education and was devoted to him. He sent her to St Petersburg with a group of sisters to study music and painting at the Academy of Fine Arts. There they formed a daughter house of the Diveyevo community. Some members of the imperial family became interested in the novices and it was through them that Father Joasaph strengthened his position at the court. He even succeeded in persuading the Tsarina to obtain from the Holy Synod the rights of a monastery for the community of Diveyevo.

In 1858 Manturov died. Joasaph now thought that he was free from all rivalry, for he counted on Motovilov being on his side. So he left Diveyevo for Nijni-Novgorod. Then, taking advantage of his absence, the sisters unanimously elected Sister Elizabeth Uchakov as their mother superior. She had come to Diveyevo in 1844 at the age of twenty-five and had attracted the community's attention by her modesty, her devotion to Father Seraphim's memory, and her spiritual and intellectual gifts. Born of a noble family, she was well educated, had studied music and chant, and had book-keeping experience. But Father Joasaph, who regarded himself as their tutor, gave her the most menial tasks. In this year 1860 she had reached the age of forty, and her humility together with her strength of character caused all the sisters to choose her for the office of superior.

In 1861 Nectary, Archbishop of Nijni-Novgorod, who was a close friend of Father Joasaph, received the order from the Holy Synod to promote the community of Diveyevo to the rank of monastery. It was now necessary to nominate a superior, because Sister Elizabeth had not yet made her monastic vows and her election was not valid in the eyes of the ecclesiastical authorities.

On 18 May 1861 Archbishop Nectary came to Diveyevo to tell the sisters that their community had been raised to the status of a monastery and that he had come to proceed with the election of a superior. Providentially his arrival coincided with that of Motovilov who, with his wife and two daughters, also arrived on the same day. He was on his

way to Moscow to place his two daughters in a boarding
school, but a wheel of his carriage was damaged during the
journey so that he had to make a detour and stop at Diveyevo. As he was driving up to his house he met blessed
Parascovia Meliukov, his wife's aunt. She told him that
she was returning from Father Seraphim's spring where she
had met Sister Glykeria, Father Joasaph's favourite, and as
that sister had approached, the water had bubbled and
tossed. 'She is the one who is causing all our trouble,' she
said, 'but the time has now come to bear witness and I must
act. "Do not be afraid to tell the whole truth," Father
Seraphim ordered me, "because as soon as you have done
so your end will come." '

When she came home Sister Parascovia lit the candles
before the icon and burned incense, to banish the powers
of evil, 'because,' she said, 'they come from all sides, climb
through the windows and push through the doors, but
Father Seraphim protects us.' Her ecstacy increased, she
saw visions, foretold the future, spoke to Father Seraphim
as though he were standing beside her: 'You remember how
you snatched me from the hay rick and set me on the
ground, as though showing me a way full of thorns and
obstacles? Well, may God's will be done!' Then she sent for
her niece, Helen Motovilov, whom she had brought up
since young Mary's death, and said goodbye to her. A little
later she was to tell Motovilov openly about her approaching
death and to remind him of his duty to go on fighting for
the truth.

While this was happening in Sister Parascovia's cell, at
.the other side of the great court blessed Pelagia, whom the
Staretz had previously told to watch over his 'orphans', was
likewise praying in great consternation. 'There's a storm
coming,' she said. Indeed, the heavens seemed to be taking
a part in events. Black clouds were massing, lightning
streaked the sky, and distant thunder rumbled. Soon the
storm broke, with torrential rain. In spite of that, Pelagia
went out into the court and, through the darkness of night,

watched from afar as by the light of torches and lanterns and with the ringing of bells Archbishop Nectary and his retinue came on their way to enter the monastery. She spent the whole night in prayer.

On the following day Archbishop Nectary sent for Sister Elizabeth who had been elected 'superior' by Father Seraphim's 'orphans' and told her to resign: she was to be sent to another monastery. When the sisters heard about this order they cried out: 'We want no other superior except Elizabeth!'

While the Archbishop was making a general inspection of the community, visiting the cells and questioning the sisters about this unexpected rebellion, the two blessed fools of Christ exerted themselves each in their own way, in the solitude of their cells. Parascovia, usually so calm and meek, had broken the glass and was calling through the window: 'Pelagia, second Seraphim, come and help me!' Pelagia was praying too, sitting on the floor. This warfare of the blessed fools affected the community profoundly. It seemed as though unseen powers were attacking the monastery and that the two saints were re-enacting in their behaviour what they were witnessing in the invisible world.

The day went on in extreme tension. The Archbishop's conscience was troubling him but he dared not go against the decision of the Holy Synod. On the evening of 19 May he told the 500 sisters to go to the refectory for the election; this was a mere formality, because the choice had been made already and Sister Glykeria was to be superior. However, 460 sisters devoted to Sister Elizabeth begged the Archbishop to let her remain superior and only 40, the followers of Father Joasaph, abstained. The Archbishop's stentorian voice and the sisters' sobs filled the refectory when Motovilov entered. He was aghast at the situation and decided to act.

The Archbishop left the room without a word. The next day he told the deacon to announce, after the Liturgy, that

Sister Glykeria had been appointed superior. Sobs and murmurs were the only response. Mother Eudoxia (she it was who had been present when the Holy Virgin appeared to Father Seraphim) could not contain herself and cried out in indignation: 'Your Excellency, do have pity on us; for we have endured persecution from Joasaph for thirty years and now you too are against us. But be sure of this, none of us will accept Glykeria!' After the Liturgy the Archbishop together with the sisters who were Joasaph's disciples went to the new superior. But the other sisters, particularly the older ones, spent the day in prayer.

During the meal, blessed Parascovia leapt out into the middle of the refectory, planting herself in front of the Archbishop, and hurled these words at him: 'O wicked and unjust judge, can you tell me where justice is to be found?' Then she added: 'If you won't give it, then the Tsar himself is going to be our judge!' The Archbishop was greatly taken aback, for he regarded Parascovia as a very holy person and he was afraid of her wrath.

Parascovia had fulfilled her mission; she returned to her cell to await her death, as the holy Staretz had predicted. Nine days after the Archbishop's departure she was to die in peace, on 1 June 1861, the feast of the Ascension. When Glykeria informed the Archbishop of her death he was overcome and could only say: 'O what a great servant of God she was!'

Then there was Pelagia, sitting by the roadside waiting for the Archbishop to pass by. When he saw her, he climbed down from the carriage and took several steps towards her. But Pelagia turned away from him. As he would not go away she stood up and calmly slapped his face. The Archbishop presented his other cheek, saying as he did so, 'All right, slap the other one too!' 'One is enough,' answered Pelagia, and she took herself off.

The Archbishop let the incident drop. This goes to show how deeply the conviction exists in Russia that the voice of God not always makes itself heard through the mouthpiece of the hierarchy, through some discreet official; but that it is sometimes heard through the 'simpletons', the 'fools' whose words and deeds, though they provoke scandal, are nevertheless manifestations of the truth.

After the election of Glykeria, the very next day, Motovilov went to Moscow. His hour had come. As soon as he arrived he sought advice from his friends. Khomiakov had just died in the cholera epidemic which had raged throughout Russia; his friend and cousin Kireyevsky had also departed, but his widow Natalie welcomed him joyfully. For she had known Father Seraphim, had been to Sarov several times, and was devastated to hear what was going on at Diveyevo. She advised Motovilov to seek out Metropolitan Philaret and give him a full account of the affair. The Metropolitan, known and respected for his justice, wisdom, and impartial judgements, was then staying at the Laura[6] of the Trinity of St Sergius where he was daily expecting the arrival of the imperial couple. The superior of the monastery was at that time Archimandrite Anthony, who had known Father Seraphim and had a great admiration for him. The Staretz had predicted that he would be made Abbot of this venerable monastery, and we recall the explanation that Father Seraphim gave him about the gift of prophecy attributed to himself. During his last visit to Sarov the Staretz had said to him as they parted: 'Don't forget my orphans!' When he heard Motovilov's story the Archimandrite went to the Metropolitan and exposed the whole affair. Then, on that very day, the Tsar and his family arrived. The next day the Metropolitan was beside His Majesty at a dinner given in his honour. Near him, at another table, some members of the court who were patrons of Joasaph were talking together. The name of Diveyevo was mentioned and the Metropolitan took advantage of the fact to tell the Tsar about the situation there. 'I myself hadn't much faith in Joasaph's words when the Tsarina told me about him', said the Tsar; and he ordered a thorough investigation to be made into what was going on at Diveyevo.

And this is what Metropolitan Philaret wrote to Metropolitan Isidore on 1 November 1861: '. . . The examiners are now making their report and you will soon be in possession of the latest facts concerning Diveyevo. It has been confirmed that the election of Glykeria was wholly arbitrary; Joasaph has behaved disgracefully . . . so I wholly approve your decision to give Bishop Nectary another diocese.'[7]

The Metropolitan also succeeded in placing the community of Diveyevo under the jurisdiction of the Archbishop of Tambov instead of that of Nijni-Novgorod. Joasaph was forbidden to set foot on the community's ground. It was wholly thanks to the action of Metropolitan Philaret that everything gradually settled down and peace reigned once more at Diveyevo. Joasaph's supporters were sent away and Mother Elizabeth was recognized as superior of the community. She took the great habit under the name of Mary, and under that name she was installed as superior of the monastery in 1862 by Bishop Theophan of Tambov.[8] So Father Seraphim's words were fulfilled: 'With the twelfth superior all will be well with you. The hemp will grow tall and strong when the darnel is pulled up.'

In 1865 Mother Mary was engaged on the building of the cathedral which had been entirely abandoned since its inauguration on the other site. Erected in the name of the Holy Trinity as Father Seraphim had wished, it was finally completed only in 1875, four years before Motovilov's death.

Motovilov in the last years of his life attained to an inner peace he had never known before, and he kept away from politics and worldly concerns. He spent most of his time on pilgrimage, and this unusual man, tall in stature with noble, virile features, long white beard and flowing hair, was often to be seen in the monasteries of vast Russia. He remained eccentric to the last. When he came to Diveyevo it was his daily custom, whatever the weather, to go round the Virgin's Path and, during the great winter frosts when the high bank flanking the moat was covered with ice, he would kneel down and, heedless of peoples' scoffing, continue his way on hands and knees.

'You're the one who is mad, Nikolka!' (that was Pelagia's name for him) said the blessed 'fool'. 'You're as mad as I am!' She was the only one who really understood him. Like her, he had fulfilled his mission in keeping the Staretz' commands and making them known to the Tsar himself, just as blessed Parascovia had foretold. And now he was ready to die.

Shortly before his death he told his wife that the Queen of Heaven had promised in a dream to bring him to a holy place which he had never visited and to show him some of God's chosen ones of whom he had never heard. On 14 January 1870 he passed peacefully away on his estate at Simbirsk, leaving his wife, two daughters and four sons. He was buried at Diveyevo as Father Seraphim had wished.

In 1927 his grave was still to be seen. Five large birch trees had sprung up on it, as a sign of his presence and that of his four sons buried with him. One of the birches had thrust its way through the middle of the gravestone and the other four rose up at the four corners.

We do not know what happened to his manuscripts in the archives of Diveyevo. There are only the extracts from them published by Father Tchichagov; as for his conversation about the Holy Spirit, that was given to the writer Nilus by Motovilov's wife, so that he could make it known.

The more one contemplates the life of Seraphim the man of God, the more evident it becomes that this constellation of rare and eccentric souls surrounding him sheds even greater light on the saint's own image, so that it stands out before us in all its reality and spiritual grandeur.

## 'SERAPHIM'S SERAPH'

Among them, we must pause and contemplate that 'fool in Christ', blessed Pelagia who, as we have seen, had so great and mysterious a role to play in the development and history of the monastery of Diveyevo.

Pelagia came to live at Diveyevo in 1837 and she chose as her dwelling-place a cell which was the only one dating from St Seraphim's day and which had escaped Ivan Tikhonovitch's demolitions. After all the afflictions she had endured from her mother and husband she did not come to Diveyevo to live an easy, pleasure-loving life. Her way of telling people the truth in no uncertain manner, without flattery, did not attract sympathy; but she even seemed to derive pleasure from the persecutions which her preposterous words and actions brought down on herself, and deliberately to provoke these persecutions by her behaviour. A fire in the monastery left some holes in the court, containing water and piles of rubble and bricks. Pelagia's daily occupation consisted of hurling bricks into the water with all her strength to fill up the holes. After this task, which seemed quite mad, she would go back to her cell in the evening, drenched through. She never lay down but spent the whole night sitting in the same corner of her cell, under the icon of the Virgin.

In 1848 her husband died of cholera and Pelagia, with her gift of intuition, was aware of it: 'He is dying, he is dying,' she exclaimed, weeping. When she became known in the community for her gift of prophecy her family took a certain interest in her and her mother came to see her, bringing presents and asking forgiveness for having ill-treated her. Pelagia only said: 'May God forgive you.'

Pilgrims coming to Sarov or Diveyevo went to see her and among them was the famous Parascovia, 'Pacha the fool' as she was called. These two 'fools of God' seemed to have something very important to discuss, but those who heard them could not make out what it was that they were saying to one another.

Towards the end of 1861, when Mother Mary became superior again, Pelagia quietened down. She hardly ever went out any more but stayed sitting in her favourite corner. She loved wild flowers and they were brought to her in profusion; she wove them into wreaths to decorate the icons and Father Seraphim's portrait. She spent the nights in prayer, shedding copious tears, so much so that her eyelids became inflamed and she could hardly see. Then came the year 1880 when Tsar Alexander II was to be assassinated.[9] 'O, if you knew what is happening!' she said. 'How unjust it is!'

She was a very humble person, patient and meek, smiling and silent in the face of injustice. She knew everything that went on in the monastery without anyone telling her. When there was talk of robbery in the neighbourhood and the doors were going to be bolted, she quietly affirmed that there was no danger for the community, 'because those whose duty it is to keep watch over it will do so.' At that moment the watchmen's voices were heard and the sisters felt reassured; but Pelagia said to thim: 'O no, not those watchmen, but the guardians to whom God has entrusted us.'

In spite of her great veneration for Father Seraphim, she never went to pray at his tomb. 'Why should I,' she said, 'since he is always here with us?' She seldom made her Communion and hardly ever went to confession, and when she was rebuked for this she simply answered: 'But Father Seraphim gave me absolution for the rest of my life.' And when the sisters became importunate Father Vassili would say: 'Leave her alone; this servant of God knows far more than you do about the ways of the Lord.'

Once, in 1882, the sister who shared her cell seemed to see, during the night, a priest and deacon coming into the cell with the Holy Gifts. She thought she was dreaming; but the dream went on, for she heard their footsteps retreating and the door being shut behind someone. She went to see what Pelagia was up to, and found her radiant with joy; the sister could not go to sleep again, but neither would Pelagia answer her questions. The sister then began watching Pelagia. 'Suddenly', she tells us, 'I heard Father Seraphim's voice, and Pelagia answering him. I could not catch the gist of the conversation but I gathered that they were talking about the community. When the voice ceased I came up and asked the favoured soul: "It really was Father Seraphim talking to you, wasn't it? I recognized his voice." But I could not get a word out of Sister Pelagia.'

Pelagia took up spinning and her work was much admired. Sometimes she was given mending which she did with great care, but occasionally she spoilt her work; that used to happen when trouble was coming. One day when she was given a cup of tea she seized the cup and, dashing out of her cell, hurled the contents in the direction of the village. We are told that at the same moment a fire broke out but that it was put out by an invisible power.

In January 1884 she began to say farewell to those who came to see her. She was manifestly failing. When the sister who lived with her lamented her approaching death, Pelagia said quietly: 'Don't cry; whoever remembers me, I will remember and, if the Lord grants me this grace, I will offer up prayer for the whole world. I shall be more use in heaven than on earth.' A few days before her death the sister heard her quietly singing the canticles of the Dormition of the Virgin: 'The angels were astonished, seeing the Virgin going up from earth to heaven.'

Two days later the same sister heard a harsh, raucous voice addressing Pelagia; the speaker seemed to be arguing with her. 'Who is talking to you in that extraordinary voice?' she asked her. She thought it was a thief whom Pelagia might let in. 'Yes,' said Pelagia, 'he is a thief, the one who steals souls!'

One evening she said: 'I want to see the stars in the sky once more!', she who no longer left her cell. But hardly had she crossed the threshold when she collapsed and had to be brought back.

During the night of 23 January, although it was winter, a storm burst, with lightning and thunderclaps. The elements seemed to be proclaiming the end. The evening before she died Pelagia made her Communion and received the sacrament of unction. At dawn on the 30th, at the age of seventy-five, she quietly passed away.[10]

They dressed her and put flowers in her hands, and the rosary that Father Seraphim had given her the first time that she came to see him. Watch was kept in her cell for three days, where she lay surrounded with candles and flowers. Then she was laid in a coffin of cyprus wood carved with cherubim, and she was carried to the church where for nine days she lay exposed to the sight of thousands of people who came from all parts to bid her farewell.

'Watch over my orphans!' Father Seraphim had said to her. Faithful to her promise, for forty-seven years she had lived at the door of her cell like a faithful watch dog, or better, like the community's angel, Seraphim's earthly seraph, armed with the flaming sword of the folly in Christ, which is a scandal to the world and wisdom for the elect.

## BLESSED PACHA

After Pelagia's death 'Pacha' succeeded her as the community's guardian. Six years before she died Pelagia had initiated her into the mysteries of their common vocation. Pacha lived to a great age, in a cottage beside the monastery gate. The sisters used to call her 'our mother'. She too drew crowds of visitors and possessed the gift of prophecy.[11] In 1913 I myself was received by her during my pilgrimage to Sarov and Diveyevo, and I still remember the amazingly penetrating gaze of her blue eyes.

Pacha died aged more than one hundred, shortly before the 1917 Revolution which she had foretold to Tsar Nicholas II in 1903, on the occasion of his visit to Diveyevo.

## NOTES

[1] This is what Ivan Tikhonovitch is sometimes called because of his artistic talents and his origin.

[2] It needs to be said that when looking at the story of Diveyevo it is hard to separate the figure of St Seraphim from those of his

137

'orphans' or of his faithful friends Manturov, Motovilov, Parascovia and Pelagia. That is why we keep returning to them.

[3] From 1830–1833.

[4] Ivan Tikhonovitch took the monastic habit under the name of Joasaph.

[5] Memoirs of N. A. Motovilov, notebooks no. 40–60 in the *Chronicles of Diveyevo*.

[6] In the early Church a colony of anchorites was called a laura. The Laura of the Holy Trinity, founded by St Sergius of Radonezh, became one of Russia's greatest monasteries.

[7] *Letters of Metropolitan Philaret* (Moscow), vol. 1, p. 127.

[8] Bishop Theophan, better known as Theophan the Recluse, who translated into Russian the *Philokalia* and *Unseen Warfare*, may be considered as a successor to St Seraphim in his watchful care over the community of Diveyevo. His spirituality constitutes a link between St Seraphim and the later nineteenth century.

[9] He abolished serfdom in Russia, which is why the Russian people called him 'the Liberator'.

[10] These facts are taken from *The Life of Blessed Pelagia of Diveyevo* written by the sister who shared her cell. Tver, 1891.

[11] Cf. *The Life of Blessed Pacha of Sarov*, Odessa 1912.

# 10

# Canonization

Years flowed by after the death of Staretz Seraphim. The stream of pilgrims steadily increased. There was talk of miracles and cures, and these were registered in Sarov's archives, certified by depositions from numerous witnesses. Water was fetched from the spring; so also was sand from the Staretz' grave, over which a chapel had been built. The people could hardly wait for the Holy Synod to declare the sanctity of the man of God.

Then in 1892 the Synod instituted an official inquiry. into the Staretz' life and miracles and appointed a special commission to deal with it.[1] Ten years later, since nothing seemed to be happening, Tsar Nicholas II, who had a great veneration for Father Seraphim, expressed the wish to see the inquiry brought to a conclusion. Through several of its members, the imperial family had experienced the power of the Staretz' intercession. A grand duchess had been healed through his prayers, and so had the Tsar's great-grandmother, the wife of Nicholas I.

It is related that in 1903 a letter was handed to Tsar Nicholas II which had been written by Father Seraphim for the 'fourth Tsar' to come to Sarov. And Nicholas was the fourth. So it was at the sovereign's instigation and in spite of opposition from some members of the Holy Synod that the commission responsible for the inquiry came to Sarov in January 1903 to proceed with the exhumation of the Staretz' body.

The cavity was opened and was found to be full of water, but the oak coffin was intact. When the lid was raised, there was the body of Seraphim, wrapped in his monastic cloak.

It had suffered the ravages of death, and the bones had become brown by the action of time and of the oak-wood. Father Seraphim's hair and beard had a reddish-brown tinge. His brass cross rested intact on his breast.[2]

The coffin was closed again and was tilted for a time, to allow the water to drain away. During the morning of 3 July it was brought to the infirmary church for the ablution of the relics. During this rite there was a scent of flowers and honey, and the Metropolitan of Moscow, Vladimir, entering the church at that moment, asked: 'What soap are you using my brothers? It seems too scented.' They showed him the ordinary soap which was used for washing the holy table at the consecration of altars, and the Metropolitan, deeply moved, made the sign of the cross, realizing where the scent came from.[3] The precious relics were deposited in a cyprus-wood reliquary which was placed in an oak coffin, a replica of the previous one.[4]

The next few days at Sarov went by in an unprecedented whirl of activity. Sheds were built and tents erected to receive the thousands of pilgrims who were arriving from all directions, having heard the news of the forthcoming canonization. Stalls and shops were set up so that everyone could be fed. And poor and sick folk were streaming along all the approaching roads, hoping to be cured.

During the morning of 17 July the procession of sisters from Diveyevo came into sight at the edge of the forest and a procession of monks from Sarov came out to meet them. Then the two processions, accompanied by an infinite number of pilgrims carrying icons and lighted candles, filled the great cathedral of the Dormition of the Virgin. At 3 o'clock in the afternoon a peal of bells announced the arrival of the imperial family. The next day, 18 July, at 5 a.m., the last Offices for the repose of Father Seraphim's soul began in all the churches of Sarov, and at 6 o'clock in the evening the great cathedral bell tolled for the beginning of Vespers, during which the Staretz was to be glorified as a saint for the first time. Everyone who had been able to get

into the cathedral, as well as those who had to stand outside, held lighted candles and the brightness of those
thousand tongues of fire was like a single flame of joy rising
to heaven. During the solemn procession of clergy from the
sanctuary to the narthex, to the sound of hymns and chants,
the celebrants followed by the imperial couple and all the
faithful made their way to the infirmary church where the
doors were wide open. The coffin containing the holy relics
was censed and placed on a litter. And so 'poor Seraphim'
was borne in solemn procession on the shoulders of bishops,
priests and of the Tsar himself. As the procession went by
some women were overcome by tears, others spread pieces
of cloth and embroidery. When the Office was over the
cathedral doors were left open all night so that the crowds
could approach the coffin.

The next morning, the anniversary of the birth of Saint
Seraphim, the relics were placed in a marble shrine with a
silver cover bearing seraphim at each corner, and then a
new procession wound through the roads of Sarov. It was
as though Father Seraphim was returning to these places
to give his blessing to all those who had come to glorify
him. He was to become one of the greatest saints to be
venerated in Russia and beyond.

Twenty years after this triumphant canonization the
Soviets occupied the monastery of Sarov and everything
was desecrated. Saint Seraphim's relics were put in a crate to
be transported, it was said, to an anti-religious museum,[5]
but it is not known whether they ever arrived there.

At one time Sarov was used as a holiday camp for dis-
abled and delinquent children but, later, the monastery
was turned into a concentration camp for deported clergy.

At this period isolated groups could still be seen coming,
at the risk of police-arrest, to fetch water from Saint
Seraphim's spring, or even some of that soil on which he
had walked.

Then in September 1927 Diveyevo was liquidated. The
sisters were expelled and they dispersed into various regions

of vast Russia. They had been able to eke out an existence working with the peasants in the village and neighbourhood or earning their living by sewing, embroidery, painting and photography.

During the years 1930–1937 the forest of Sarov became a lumber camp and political deportees worked there, floating the timber down the rivers Satis and Sarovka. An engineer who spent several years of forced labour there relates how, on the days when they could go outside the barbed wire for walks in the forest under observation, they used to meet old men and women making their way to Seraphim's spring under the pretext of gathering mushrooms. Some of them told the engineer that amazing things sometimes happened in this district.[6]

It seems that the forest of Sarov has now become a 'forbidden zone' but the writer Nilus records the words he heard from the lips of the superior of the monastery of Diveyevo, Mother Mary,[7] at the time of Father Seraphim's canonization: 'We must now wait for Father Seraphim's return to Diveyevo.' To Nilus's astonishment she added: 'How are we to know, sinners that we are, whether this will happen visibly or invisibly? The relics of the saints will remain hidden for some time, but I am convinced that one day our dear Staretz will come back to us.'

## NOTES

[1] Inquiries were made in 28 departments of European Russia, and in Siberia as well, and about a hundred miracles were registered.

[2] We have taken these details from the book *Saint Seraphim of Sarov* (Tallin 1939) by Father Dimitri Troitski, who witnessed the exhumation.

[3] Ibid.

[4] 'The divine life, which becomes the inheritance of their whole body, does not leave the Saints at the moment of death, but continues to be manifest in their bodies. This is the very foundation of the veneration of relics: "Glorify the holy tombs of the Saints," Palamas

teaches, "and, if they are there, the relics of their bones, for the grace of God has not abandoned them." ' *A Study of Gregory Palamas* by John Meyendorff (London, Faith Press 1964), p. 176.

5 Father D. Troitski speaks of the relics being brought to a Moscow museum in his pamphlet published on the occasion of the 35th anniversary of the canonization of Father Seraphim (Paris 1938), p. 23.

6 Testimony recorded by a publication of Holy Trinity Monastery for the 50th anniversary of the canonization of St Seraphim of Sarov, Jordanville, U.S.A., 1953.

7 Mother Mary died on 19 August 1904.

### Publisher's Note

[The relics of St. Seraphim and other saints were seized by the Communists with the intention of displaying them at an anti-religious exhibition, which never took place. We now know that the relics were taken to Kazan Cathedral in Leningrad, which became a museum of atheism. There they lay hidden for nearly 70 years.

In 1990, the Church was given access to the Kazan Cathedral, and the relics were found in the crypt. A label identified the relics as those of St. Seraphim. Since Sarov is still off-limits due to security reasons, the relics were brought to Diveyevo Convent in 1991 in a 450-mile-long procession which stopped at many churches along the way.]

# Conclusion

The rediscovery, through St Seraphim, of the real presence of the Holy Spirit active in the world and in mankind today marks a renewal of the traditional Orthodox thought of the nineteenth century. The one essential for us to grasp is that for the holy Staretz the present world is not really another world, different from the one we call the life of heaven, but one in which the Kingdom of God may already be shining and the Holy Spirit already acting according to the amazing richness of his gifts. Through the discipline of his life and the ardour of his prayers Saint Seraphim had here below attained the possibility of realizing the true 'likeness' of God and through his own personality showing this to others. This great figure of the nineteenth century had grown to a dimension reaching far beyond his era and the mentality of his surroundings where scientific enlightenment had already begun to lay hold of the Russian soul. According to him, man is neither a product of matter nor a spirit imprisoned in the bondage of the body, but a being called to establish the sovereignty of God and his Kingdom over his material body and over his soul as well in their indestructible union. He expressed in his teaching the profound conviction that the seed of resurrection in Christ which is sown in baptism cannot be destroyed by death. Moreover the Church sings on his festival: 'Rejoice, O blessed Seraphim, with the joy of the Kingdom which you have already tasted on earth!' Therefore we are to believe that the paschal greeting which Seraphim used to give his visitors was no mere form of politeness but expressed his own deepest conviction; likewise those Easter hymns which he was singing during the last hours of his life were the proclamation of his burning faith in the risen Christ. He was already living this new life which Christ brought and which was even now quickened in his heart.[1] Moreover the words, teaching and experience of the holy Staretz constitute a precious witness to the deifying power of the Holy Spirit operating in man right into our own days.

It is well known how important to the Russian people was the role of those men of God living a like spirituality to St Seraphim's.[2] There was the Optino hermitage, for instance, where, as we know, for nearly a century (1828–1921) Russian intellectuals such as Dostoievski, Vladimir Soloviev, Ivan Kireyevski and others went to renew their strength. And was not Dostoievski seeking to depict a hermitage in his *Brothers Karamazov* and a staretz in the person of Zosima when he wrote: 'You would be surprised if I were to tell you that it is through the prayers of these humble seekers of solitude and silence that we shall find the salvation of Russia.' Now we know that Staretz Seraphim exercised the powers of the deifying grace of his priesthood; we know this because of the importance he laid on the sacraments of baptism and of the Eucharist. 'It is in the Spirit that rites and sacraments acquire their true function and their sole *raison d'être* which is to bring the faithful into deifying union with God.'[3]

Defining startzi as 'organs of the Holy Spirit' Paul Evdokimov goes as far as to regard Saint Seraphim as 'a living icon of the very heart of Orthodoxy'.[4] During the great ordeal, the disciples of the startzi were scattered; they swarmed over the steppes and forests of vast Russia, so that their voices were heard beyond her frontiers, and perhaps it is they who are bearing witness throughout the world today to the transfiguration of man through the Holy Spirit.

## NOTES

[1] 'Those who attain as far as they possibly can to Christ's hidden life are raised up in the "first resurrection",' Gregory Palamas tells

us. According to him 'the "resurrection of the soul" was no less than an anticipation of the bodily and general resurrection on the Last Day. It was an earnest of the new life, brought by Christ, and already active in the heart of man.' *A Study of Gregory Palamas* by John Meyendorff, p. 155.

[2] Igor Smolitch, *Moines de la Sainte Russie*, ed. Mame, 1967.

[3] B. Bobrinskoy, 'Présence réelle et communion eucharistique', in *Revue des sciences philosophiques et theologiques*' 1969, pp. 9–13.

[4] Paul Evdokimov, 'Saint Seraphim of Sarov: An Icon of Orthodox Spirituality' in *The Ecumenical Review*, vol. XV, No. 3, April 1963.

# Sources

A complete biography of Saint Seraphim of Sarov does not yet exist; this would be almost impossible until there can be a critical edition of the archives and material concerned.

The main sources available to the various authors for the reconstruction of the key events of the holy Staretz' life were the memories and testimonies of his contemporaries, the monks of Sarov, the nuns of Diveyevo, the priest of their churches Father Vassili Sadovski, the friends and confidants of the man of God, Michael Manturov, and Nicholas Motovilov. Their depositions were partly collected by Father Leonard Tchitchagov and published for the first time in 1896 at Moscow under the title, *Chronicles of the Monastery of Seraphim-Diveyevo*. A second edition came out in 1903 at St Petersburg.

Following the order of the *Chronicles*, we can now list the various sources from which we ourselves have drawn:

*Notebooks 1 and 2:* The reports by the nuns of Diveyevo on the foundation of the monastery and on the Staretz, Hieromonk Seraphim.

*Notebook 3:* Authentic information given by N. A. Motovilov of the two monasteries of Diveyevo and of his cure by Father Seraphim.

*Notebook 4:* Accounts of the monastery of Diveyevo taken from the notes of Archpriest Vassili Sadovski and Nicholas Motovilov.

*Notebook 5:* Description of the life of the monastery of Diveyevo, composed by order of Mgr Modest, Bishop of Nijni-Novgorod and Arzamas in 1885 for the Consistory.

*Notebook 6:* Accounts of the monastery of Diveyevo from the notes of Archpriest Vassili Sadovski, Nicholas Motovilov and Michael Manturov: a) Foundation by Staretz Seraphim of the second community of the Mill in the village of Diveyevo; b) Building of the windmill in the monastery; c) Michael Manturov; d) Building of the churches of the Nativity; e) 81 accounts by the older nuns of Father Seraphim's sayings.

*Notebooks 7 and 8:* On the subject of blessed Pacha of Sarov.

*Notebook 9:* Life of blessed Pelagia.

*Notebook 10:* Stories of Parascovia and Mary Meliukov.

*Notebook 11:* (Confused account) Life of the nun Helen, in the world H. V. Manturov.

*Notebooks 12 and 13:* Short description and information about Diveyevo.

*Notebooks 14 and 15:* Short account of the cathedral of the Trinity at Diveyevo.

*Notebook 16:* Death of Mother Agatha and founding of the community of the Mill.

*Notebook 17:* About Parascovia Meliukova.

*Notebook 18:* Memories of the life of Staretz Anthony.

*Notebook 19:* Information about blessed Natalie.

*Notebook 20:* 30 accounts of cures by Father Seraphim.

*Notebook 21:* Account of the two last days of Parascovia's life.

*Notebook 22:* (Confused) Accounts of Father Seraphim and his miracles, also of the old nuns, by V. A. Karamzin.

*Notebooks 23–28:* Chronicles of the first superiors of the community of Diveyevo and accounts of the miraculous virtue of Father Seraphim's water.

*Notebooks 29–38:* (Confused) Accounts of Father Seraphim and his miracles, of Manturov, and of the first superiors of Diveyevo.

*Notebook 34:* Letters and notes of the chief of police Paul Bettling.

*Notebook 35:* Old papers of Michael Manturov concerning the purchase of the land and the building of the church of the Nativity.

*Notebook 36:* (Confused) Notes of V. A. Karamzin of Father Seraphim's miracles.

*Notebook 37:* Some comments on the book *Accounts of the Ascetic Life of Staretz Seraphim* by a neighbour of the Sarov hermitage and the community of Diveyevo. (We may have here Ivan Tikhonovitch's book which was published in 1849 at St Petersburg.)

*Notebook 38:* Information about Father Seraphim given by the monastery of Slobada of Viatka with a copy of the letter from Agaphangel, Bishop of Viatka.

*Notebook 39:* Letters and telegrams referring to Abbess Mary's jubilee.

*Notebooks 40–60:* N. Motovilov's notes, which were discovered in 1903 by the writer Nilus in the granary at Diveyevo. In the *Chronicles* published by Father Tchitchagov it is said that N. Motovilov thought it too soon to publish certain revelations which Father Seraphim had disclosed to him, but that he hoped to publish them later.

One might add that a life of Saint Seraphim, based on the *Chronicles* of Archimandrite Tchitchagov, arranged by L. Denissov, was published in 1904 at Moscow. In this book the author has published the notes of N. Motovilov which appeared in the *Journal of Moscow*, and also Father Seraphim's *Instructions* taken from the notes made by monks of Sarov.

# A Select Bibliography
# of Works in English

*Early Fathers from the Philokalia*, tr. Kadloubovsky and Palmer. Faber and Faber 1954.

*Flame in the Snow*, I. de Beausobre. Constable 1945.

*On the Invocation of the Name of Jesus*, a Monk of the Eastern Church. Fellowship of St Alban and St Sergius 1950.

*The Mystical Theology of the Eastern Church*, V. Lossky. Clarke 1957.

'Orthodox Spirituality and Protestant and Anglican Spirituality', L. Bouyer in *A History of Christian Spirituality*, vol. 3. Burns & Oates 1969.

'Saint Seraphim, an Icon of Orthodox Spirituality', P. Evdokimov in *Ecumenical Review*, vol. XV, no. 3, 1963.

*Saint Seraphim of Sarov*, V. Zander. Fellowship of St Alban and St Sergius 1968.

*A Study of Gregory Palamas*, J. Meyendorff. Faith Press 1964.

*The Way of a Pilgrim*, tr. R. M. French. SPCK 1973.

*Writings from the Philokalia on Prayer of the Heart*, tr. Kadloubovsky and Palmer. Faber and Faber 1951.